"THIS GREAT
TRIUMVIRATE
OF PATRIOTS"

Also by Harry Barnard
"Eagle Forgotten," The Life of John Peter Altgeld
Rutherford B. Hayes and His America
Independent Man, The Life of Senator James Couzens
Along the Way (with Preston Bradley)

*The Inspiring Story Behind Lorado Taft's
Chicago Monument to
George Washington, Robert Morris and
Haym Salomon*

"THIS GREAT
TRIUMVIRATE
OF PATRIOTS"

by HARRY BARNARD

FOLLETT PUBLISHING COMPANY
1010 West Washington Blvd.
Chicago, Illinois 60607

ISBN 0-695-80272-0

Library of Congress card catalog number: 72-162791

First printing

THE GOVERNMENT OF THE UNITED STATES
WHICH GIVES TO BIGOTRY NO SANCTION—TO PERSECUTION
NO ASSISTANCE—REQUIRES ONLY THAT THEY WHO LIVE UNDER
ITS PROTECTION SHOULD DEMEAN THEMSELVES AS GOOD CITIZENS
IN GIVING IT ON ALL OCCASIONS THEIR EFFECTUAL SUPPORT
PRESIDENT GEORGE WASHINGTON 1790

— —statement on the base of the
George Washington— Robert Morris— Haym Salomon
Monument in Heald Square, Chicago

CONTENTS

PREFACE

One of America's most significant memorials is the Chicago monument on which the master American sculptor, Lorado Taft, was working at the time of his death. It was completed from his design in faithful accord with his overall concept and in a very real sense stands as his last creation. As I know from meeting with him at the time, Mr. Taft envisioned the George Washington-Robert Morris-Haym Salomon Monument as an artistic and patriotic work that would form an especially happy capstone for his long and fruitful career.

Although or perhaps because he was markedly patrician in heritage, in personality, and in instincts, Lorado Taft was of that breed of *true* American who took seriously the traditional principles of American democracy. *Noblesse oblige* was a natural governing principle with him extended to all regardless of their national origin, creed, or color just as it was to associates and students at his famous Midway Studio adjacent to the University of Chicago. The nobility of his creations reflects his own nobility, but it is a nobility reminiscent of a Washington and a Jefferson, also of an Emerson, a Brandeis, and a Roosevelt—one that is wholly congenial and not at all paradoxical with American egalitarianism, the essence of the democratic promise of equal opportunity for all.

In a letter to Barnet Hodes, leading spirit in sponsorship of the monument, President Franklin D. Roosevelt referred to Washington, Morris, and Salomon with the phrase that gives this book its title, "this great triumvirate of patriots." It *is* a great triumvirate, not simply because Washington is there but for what is pregnantly suggested by the inclusion of two men of the American Revolution not usually emphasized in ordinary history books. Therein lies the great point of the Taft monument and the story of why Hodes and fellow members of the Patriotic Foundation of Chicago labored so zealously to make the monument possible. Morris, a businessman of Anglo-Saxon Protestant heritage, and Salomon, a businessman of East European and Jewish background, symbolize on the monument a truth that is as important now in anticipation of the 200th anniversary of the American Revolution as it was in the founding period of the United States. It is that Jew as well as gentile, businessman as well as soldier, laborer as well as employer, commoner as well as landowner—in short, people of all social positions, creeds, and origins—were among the founders of the American republic. Enfolded in this truth is the story told here, set down as a contribution toward fuller understanding by the present generation of the kind of America the founding fathers intended to create.

H. B.

1

A Pleasant Open Space

Four of Chicago's famed streets almost meet at Heald Square—State Street, Wabash Avenue, East South Water Street, and Wacker Drive. With the Chicago River and glamorous Michigan Avenue nearby there is an unexpected and pleasant open space in the midst of the crowded bustle of the downtown area.

All around within easy eyesight and suggestive of a backdrop for some magnificently staged drama are skyscraping buildings. They include the new Equitable building, the newer IBM building, the stark square home of Encyclopaedia Britannica, the romantic tower complex of *The Chicago Tribune* and its sister newspaper *Chicago Today*, the gleaming white Wrigley building, a great oblong that houses *The Chicago Sun-Times* and *The Chicago Daily News*, the fascinating twin towers of Marina City, the immense fortress-like Merchandise Mart.

In the vicinity south of the river are the new United

of America building, the North American Life building, Oxford House and Executive House, the interestingly lean Lincoln Tower (formerly Mather Tower), the classic-designed Stone Container building. Just across from the open space is a reminder of things spiritual, the modernistic downtown Christian Science Church.

To the north on Michigan Avenue as part of the backdrop stands the 100-story John Hancock building. It pierces the nearby sky, presiding over the whole like some unbending magistrate. Its name—John Hancock —recalls not only a great insurance enterprise but also a great American Revolutionary patriot, fittingly so in relation to a Revolutionary War monument.

The open space where the four streets converge is welcome relief from the restless Chicago exuberance represented by the conglomerate units of the backdrop. In spring and summer vari-colored tulips bloom; stone benches extend an uncommon invitation to rest. More of a triangle than a square, Heald Square was named as a tribute to the commander of old Fort Dearborn, a miniscule military outpost on the river during the War of 1812. From that outpost, in the usual accounts, came Chicago—first a village, then a town, and finally a mammoth city on Lake Michigan's shore and along both banks of the river. The Chicago River, incidentally, now flows not into the lake as orthodox rivers are expected to do but, for reasons of civic sanitation, *out* of the lake, one token of the city's characteristic boldness and vigor.

Did Chicago really stem from the Indian-haunted log cabins that were Fort Dearborn? In larger context the answer is negative. It may be successfully argued that Chicago as a metropolis of the American continent— perhaps the most American of all America's great centers—had its real growth inevitably determined earlier than the War of 1812, that its growth was determined in the 1770's when the thirteen colonies broke away from Great Britain's colonial, monarch-ruled, England-centered empire. Among other things the success of the Americans' thrust for independence meant the opening up of the American West. Chicago's destiny was to become the leading city of that West.

So it is appropriate that Heald Square, instead of marking only incidents associated with Fort Dearborn, is the site of a monument that eloquently recalls a more inclusive period of America's history, the American Revolution.

Being already a people of many origins and strains—Jews and Christians, believers and atheists, whites and blacks, Nordics and Slavs, Continental Europeans (West, Central, Eastern, and Southern) as well as Anglo-Saxons—the American people did more than repudiate absentee British rule and its taxation without representation. They also gave humanity one of the great documents of world history, the American Declaration of Independence, and later the Bill of Rights as amendments to the United States Constitution. Thus was assured a form of government that ever since has been a model for humane and enlightened democratic government in every region of the globe.

Other revolutions mark world history but most are associated with cruelty and disillusionment. The revolution that produced the Declaration of Independence and the Bill of Rights continues after two centuries to be recalled as the event that brought forth a nation of dignity, hope, and glory. The story cannot be recalled too often either in words or in bronze to inspire all later generations.

If a picture is worth a thousand words, as the Chinese proverb puts it, a monument worthy of the American Revolution may be better than a thousand historical texts and documents. A monument that does artistic and thematic justice to this period of American history would have to be a significant creation. It would have to be majestic in its image and also instantly expressive of the basic ideas it is designed to project.

The monument in Chicago's Heald Square is such a creation. And it not only communicates a great story but also has a meaningful story of its own.

2
Symbolic Unity

Like the story told by the monument in Heald Square the story told *of* the monument is itself one of drama. The pages that follow not only describe the how and the why of the monument in that pleasant open space but attempt to sharpen appreciation of the political and social goals of America.

Concepts of unity projected symbolically by the monument are vitally important to the health of American society today, especially when a desirable unity of the nation behind basic principles is threatened by divisive elements and ideologies. Harmony must of necessity exist among the ethnic and religious groups that make up and made America. To a large extent harmony is the determining factor for whether or not the American experiment is to continue "as the last best hope," to quote Lincoln, for a well-ordered, responsive, working democracy.

After all, the main glory of the nation that was born

of the American Revolution on the North American continent lies not in technological attainments nor in material successes, great as these have been. The main glory derives from social and political ideals—those already established and those still to be implemented in accord with the inspired vision of the Founding Fathers, who were the patriots of the nation's formative era.

America today is mainly cities—and there are idealistic highpoints in the histories of cities just as there are in the lives of individuals. Such are times when better selves or oversouls, to use an Emersonian term, come to the top above ordinary, work-a-day, merely self-serving activity.

The Heald Square monument by the impulse behind it as well as by its permanent message represents such a time in Chicago's history. In contrast to much that goes on in every big city as the inevitable concomitant of urban life and struggle, motivation and purpose of contributors to the memorial, save for justifiable personal gratification, were purely civic and patriotic in the highest and most wholesome sense. Thus there was brought into being a fine object of art bearing the honored name of Lorado Taft and eloquently illuminating a chapter of hopeful civic and national history.

3
Triumvirate of Patriots

The monument in Heald Square standing on its massive polished mahogany marble base weighs forty-six tons. A major feature is the striking sculptured representation of George Washington.

Wearing his familiar commander-in-chief campaign clothes and the equally familiar Continental three-cornered cocked hat, he stands sturdy and dependable more than eleven feet tall. Manly physique is matched by a strong face modeled after the famous Houdon sculpture. The remarkably lifelike bronze figure is enriched by the greenish-blue patina of the weathering process—so welcomed by sculptors—which has gone on through the years since the monument was erected during the fall of 1941.

Reflecting the true situation that the War of Independence was not a one-man affair but included many other patriots, Washington properly does not stand alone. Two other men are presented, tall yet less tall than their

7

commander-in-chief. On Washington's right is Robert Morris; on Washington's left is Haym Salomon.

Joining the figures of these other patriots with Washington's—a startling combination to some—gives the monument its official name, "The George Washington—Robert Morris—Haym Salomon Monument of Chicago." At times the monument is referred to as "The Haym Salomon Monument."

That short title is a well-meant, pardonable inaccuracy, and in a certain context is not so inaccurate. For it *was* Haym Salomon's role—a symbolic role in the time of the Revolution—that sparked the creation of this monument. The intent was to make the important point that America was and is a land of many ethnic strains.

Obviously, much of the news of this monument concerns the fact that it *does* honor the name Salomon. It is a name worth remembering among patriots of the American Revolution, yet it is a name that was usually omitted from history books or reference works.

Obviously, too, Washington's role in the Revolution and the critical period immediately afterward is hardly news. Striking in its grandeur, yes; a cause for continuing admiration, yes; but not news. Washington's role is legend, taught to all Americans in one way or another from kindergarten days on. To some extent that is also true of Robert Morris, superintendent of finance of the Continental government.

But Haym Salomon? His was a name more easily associated with Old Testament figures than with leaders at America's birth. However, because of the monument in Heald Square, it has become more familiar as an American name. *Who Was Who in America,* as one example, now devotes to his biographical sketch space nearly equivalent to that of Morris and almost as much as is given Washington himself.

A meaningful day: part of the throng at dedication of the monument in Heald Square on Bill of Rights Day, 1941.

A hand of each of his companions is held by Washington in friendly, cooperative clasp. The trio is linked, strong, purposeful, dedicated men with shared ideals—accent on "together." Their general style and look convey what they were—representative Americans of their era.

Two were of Anglo-Saxon heritage, Washington, the near-aristocratic landowner and military genius; Robert Morris, the businessman organizer of great commercial ventures and important government and private financial affairs. The third was of Polish-Jewish heritage, Haym Salomon. He is an exemplary model for all the immigrants of various strains and creeds who populated America before, during, and after the Revolution.

These immigrants form a population that has given America its most significant characteristic, cultural pluralism, that is, a culture of polyglot peoples living and working together. *When they are being truly American,* they are living and working in harmony as the three figures on the monument suggest. "This great triumvirate of patriots," President Franklin D. Roosevelt called them.

4

Base of the Monument

Deeply cut into the front of the foundation in tall, chaste letters are words set down by Washington when he served as the Nation's first and only unanimously elected President, words in line with the monument's theme of cultural pluralism.

THE GOVERNMENT OF THE UNITED STATES WHICH GIVES TO BIGOTRY NO SANCTION, TO PERSECUTION NO ASSISTANCE, REQUIRES ONLY THAT THEY WHO LIVE UNDER ITS PRO-TECTION SHOULD DEMEAN THEMSELVES AS GOOD CITIZENS IN GIVING IT ON ALL OCCA-SIONS THEIR EFFECTUAL SUPPORT

PRESIDENT GEORGE WASHINGTON 1790

On the back of the base that stretches nearly twenty-four feet across, seven and a half feet in height, and eighteen feet in width there is another meaningful message. A bronze plaque nine feet across and four feet from top to bottom shows in bas-relief an assemblage of people grouped around a seated Goddess of Liberty.

This assemblage depicts yet again the major theme of the monument. The infinite variety of Americans living together as a nation. From the very beginning all races and creeds participated actively in the upbuilding of America. So meaningfully drawn are the numerous figures that the viewer at once recognizes workers, tradesmen, professionals; white people, black people, brown people; East Europeans and West Europeans; young and old; some fairly well off, many poor with only the meager possessions they carry.

". . . To Bigotry No Sanction . . ."—George Washington's famous affirmation of America's creed of tolerance is shown as chiseled into the base of the monument to him and his co-patriots. His statement expresses the basic theme of the monument.

ROBERT MORRIS · GEORGE WASHINGTON · HAYM SALOMO

★ ★ ★

THE GOVERNMENT OF THE UNITED STATES
WHICH GIVES TO BIGOTRY NO SANCTION · TO PERSECUTION
NO ASSISTANCE · REQUIRES ONLY THAT THEY WHO LIVE UNDER
ITS PROTECTION SHOULD DEMEAN THEMSELVES AS GOOD CITIZENS
IN GIVING IT ON ALL OCCASIONS THEIR EFFECTUAL SUPPORT·
PRESIDENT GEORGE WASHINGTON 1790

★ ★ ★

The Goddess of Liberty holds a torch in classic portrayal as she welcomes them to America's shores, reiterating the message of the Statue of Liberty in New York harbor in the memorable lines by Emma Lazarus:

> Give me your tired, your poor,
> Your huddled masses yearning to breathe free,
> The wretched refuse of your teeming shore.
> Send these, the homeless, tempest-tossed to me,
> I lift my lamp beside the golden door.

In fact, the two monuments are complementary—each conveying the characteristic American message of liberty and its related ideals.

This bronze placque on the base of the monument, at the rear, expresses the Spirit of Liberty that drew to America people of many origins. It amplifies the meaning of the collaboration of George Washington, Robert Morris and Haym Salomon.

Recognizing that there can never be true liberty and freedom in any nation without mutual respect for and by its component peoples, the designer further accentuated the ideals of the George Washington–Robert Morris–Haym Salomon monument on a tablet of bronze placed on the highest of three steps that ascend at the front of the marble base. The message is stated so simply that all who read may understand:

> Symbol of American Tolerance and Unity and of the Cooperation of People of All Races and Creeds in the Upbuilding of the United States.

Also on this third-step tablet are written certain basic facts as to how and when the monument came into being:

> This monument designed by Lorado Taft and completed by Leonard Crunelle was presented to the City of Chicago by The Patriotic Foundation of Chicago.
>
> Honorary Chairman
>
> The Mayor of Chicago   Edward J. Kelly
>
> Co-Chairmen
>
> Barnet Hodes   Albert A. Sprague
>
> Treasurer
>
> Laurence H. Armour
>
> Dedicated on the 150th Anniversary of the Ratification of the American Bill of Rights
>
> December 15, 1941

Behind the basic, physical description is a story of civic statesmanship, of devotion to ideals and ideas that in itself is worth knowing. No more than other creations, monuments do not spring full blown into exis-

Leonard Crunelle, associate of Lorado Taft, is shown putting finishing touches on the head of Washington. Looking on, left to right, are Barnet Hodes, Paul H. Douglas and Mrs. Douglas, Lorado Taft's daughter.

tence by themselves. Great ones like that in Heald Square come into being because of monumental—an intended pun—efforts by dedicated individuals in overcoming obstacles that would discourage men of lesser dedication and conviction.

One example is the great Washington Monument, the towering shaft in the national capitol. For years it stood half-completed. So did the Statue of Liberty until Emma Lazarus' verse, *The New Collosus*, inspired a popular money-raising campaign which made completion possible. The basic story was similar for the creation and completion of the Lincoln Memorial in Springfield, Grant's Tomb in New York City, and many another monument to memorialize national ideals or leaders who symbolize the ideals.

Personal profit is not involved. Hence the motivation must be wholly patriotic, the goal highly prized. This stance is not easy to stimulate when large effort and expense are required. The monument in Heald Square encountered unexpected obstacles, apathy, even outright opposition. But at last came the triumph of general acceptance, then enthusiasm, creation, and finally dedication.

5
Patriotic Foundation of Chicago

As embossed in the bronze tablet on its front steps, the George Washington–Robert Morris–Haym Salomon Monument was an unconditional and generous gift to Chicago and its people from the Patriotic Foundation of Chicago.

The Foundation, a continuing public-spirited, not-for-profit organization, was chartered by the State of Illinois in 1936. Each generation must be reminded of the value of American ideals—and more than once during each generation. To do its part in this regard was the underlying purpose of the Patriotic Foundation. It was organized during a critical period, a climactic point in history, when it was especially vital that Americans be reminded with dramatic force of the basic principles of their governmental system and of their society as a whole.

Social scientists understand, as did the Founding Fathers, that democratic principles and ideals are never self-perpetuating. Many Americans when in the grip of undisciplined emotional disturbance in periods of crisis or for the sake of some passing, assumed advantage are prone to disregard freedom's principles. American history frequently has been punctuated with temporary deviations from the democratic thrust, episodes of bigotry, of repression of minorities, of demagogue-inspired hatred of foreigners, of prejudice against Catholics or Jews, of contempt for intellectuals, and of open calls for suspension of the Constitutional safeguards including the Bill of Rights. In the 1950's, Chief Justice Earl Warren was able to comment with apparent justification that he doubted whether the Bill of Rights would receive majority backing if put to a vote at that time.

The world in 1936 was ostensibly at peace, that is, if the absence of shooting war meant peace. Franklin Delano Roosevelt, an inspiring democratic-minded leader, was the nation's President. That year the voters overwhelmingly retained him in the White House as he wound up the first of his history-packed four terms. Democracy, American style, seemed unchallengeable as a stable form of government even though the world's wealthiest country still suffered from socio-economic dislocations accompanying the great depression that had followed the stock market crash of October 1929.

Especially did democracy appear to be unassailable in view of the remarkable social reforms that Roosevelt's New Deal had introduced. These included unemployment insurance, old-age pensions, home loans, public works for putting jobless folk on payrolls, farm subsidies, bank-deposit insurance, and others. Democratic government in 1936 seemed to be proving itself healthy and in accord with the Founding Fathers' seminal concepts for government that would guarantee its citizens their "unalienable Rights [of] Life, Liberty, and the pursuit of Happiness." And seeming to remain in

"This great trimvirate of patriots" was Franklin Roosevelt's phrase. He was shown the model by Barnet Hodes, 1937. At right, Governor Horner and Senator Dietrich.

sight were the constitutional goals, to "establish Justice, insure domestic Tranquillity ... promote the general Welfare, and secure the Blessings of Liberty to ourselves and our Posterity."

But the somber reality of things in the world at large as well as in the United States was different. The very need for Roosevelt's expression of courage—"The only thing we have to fear is fear itself"—underscored a general malaise. The usually optimistic American people did not escape its blight.

In fact, the picture of a world at peace in 1936 was delusion; devastating global war was already in the offing. The feeling that democracy in the United States existed without serious internal as well as external challenge was delusion also; a good many Americans of high status were publicly doubting democracy's desirability. At least one prominent United States Senator, Pennsylvania's David Reed, openly expressed appreciation for dictatorship. He praised the supposed efficiency of dictators for the way they ran railroads and controlled social discontent. He was not alone in that myopic view.

Doubters of democracy included men and women of substance who beat the drums for their loyalty to Americanism. They spoke and wrote vigorously, some in publications of wide circulation which they controlled, of their own self-proclaimed one-hundred percent Americanism, insinuating that Americans who did not share their antidemocratic views were subversive or worse. Their curious brand of Americanism was more akin to loyalty for the king by Tories during the American Revolution than to loyalty for America shown by leaders like George Washington, Robert Morris, and Haym Salomon.

By 1936 Nazism was festering, boiling in Germany under the demagogue Hitler. So too was monolithic Communism in Russia under Stalin. Their openly antidemocratic, antihumanistic poisons were creeping and seeping into other parts of the world; into France, that land of "Liberty, Fraternity, and Equality"; also, under the Black Shirt Oswald Moseley into England, the home of common law and the Magna Charta; even into the United States. Active there were Nazi Bundists, revived racialists and assorted Ku Kluxers, Father Coughlins, Newton Jenkinses, and Huey Longs.

In particular, Nazism found allies in the Arab lands. It left a hostile heritage of explosive nature there to confront the world three decades later, just as Soviet ideology would leave ugly posterity in dominated Czechoslovakia and Hungary and in erupting Asia. Although posed as enemies of Communism, German Nazis stimulated in the Soviets emulation of vicious anti-Semitism, revival of the pogroms of the Czarist autocracy. Anti-Semitism became a part of Soviet culture and extended later to an unnatural, cynical alliance with Arab demagogues in hostility to the new Jewish state of Israel.

For the Jews in Europe—always the scapegoats of antidemocratic tendencies, their persecution signalling persecution of all minorities and of all liberal elements —the rise of Nazism meant destruction on a scale unequaled in world history. Its savagery exceeded even the cruelty of the prebiblical Egyptian bondage, the Polish and Russian pogroms, the bloodletting of the Roman conquests, or the Crusades. A new but darker Dark Age was Europe's condition. As in a holocaust, six million men, women, and children whose only crime was their Jewish lineage would be slaughtered, with other millions also slaughtered for the crime of not being German, or in the case of the Russian Ukraine of not being Russian.

In Italy arrogant, brutal Fascism was riding high under the self-centered Mussolini, who was only semicomic in his strutting. Fascism boasted of its doctrinal hostility toward outmoded and sissified democracy. Like Hitler and Stalin the Fascist leader saw dictatorship and the fuehrer principle as the wave of the future.

In Japan a clique of antidemocratic warlords mesmerized their assumed Godly emperor with religious concepts of conquest. They were guiding a potentially beautiful and constructive nation toward war of unashamed, bloody cruelty in the Pacific and on the Asian mainland.

Nazism, Fascism, and the Japanese mystique of conquest all had in common an enmity for the ideals on which America was founded. Deep set in their warped philosophy was antagonism toward the Judaeo-Christian concepts of social justice and human dignity.

Indeed, the Nazis were as insanely hostile toward

Christians as they were toward people in all lands who were Jews or merely had Jewish forebears. Jews, but not Jews alone, were marked as victims. All non-Aryans were to be literally exterminated because they were considered inferior, scum. The Nazi open boast was a goal of mass murder, genocide. This doctrine expressed in Hitler's book, *Mein Kampf*, was so demented, so outrageous, so incredible in its evil that rational people naively refused to accept it as seriously to be implemented. Decent people refused to recognize that in the supposedly enlightened twentieth century new Hamans, new Neroes, and new Torquemadas had returned as Hitler and his associates.

In this climate Nazis, Fascists, and Japanese warlords generated an enormous pollution that threatened most of what Western civilization had achieved in the long march of history away from barbarianism and cruel prejudices toward decency and humanity. World War II would break out in Europe in 1939—as the Chicago monument was being shaped for its bronze casting by Lorado Taft's successor. The United States would become involved in December 1941—when the monument was unveiled and dedicated in Heald Square. It was a war characterized by the promised genocide of non-Aryan peoples in Europe, not only the Jewish Europeans, but Poles, Slavs, Greeks, Armenians, and others who were senselessly despised by the Hitler-led Nazis, a people gone mad.

Perhaps never before in recorded history was mindless, subhuman racial and credal prejudice riding so high, so brutally, as in that storm-tossed generation of the 1930's when, like a tiny candle in ominous darkness, the Patriotic Foundation launched its work.

6

Message of the Monument

In that time of the monument's genesis there had to be a brighter side to the picture if the Nazis, assorted Fascists, and Japanese warlords were to be defeated. And there was a brighter side in the enlightened acceptance of people of all strains, including Jews, as full-fledged respected citizens in nations outside the Nazi orbit.

In France Leon Blum of Jewish background was premier, and none except later French Nazis or Vichyites questioned his patriotism.

In the United States the acceptance of minorities was firmly based (save only the masses of Negroes, whose time had not yet arrived, although it was beginning to dawn in the North). There had occurred spurts of anti-Semitism as during the revival of the Ku-Klux Klan in the 1920's, but on balance the nation as a whole had rejected that social disease. By the 1930's it was no longer considered a matter of extraordinary interest for citizens of Jewish faith or heritage to be part of the mainstream of American life, properly trusted and honored in all spheres, without giving up their Judaism. Two of the most revered members of the Supreme Court in 1936 were Jews, Justice Louis Dembitz Brandeis, called a modern day Isaiah by Franklin Roosevelt, and the scholarly, saint-like Benjamin Nathan Cardozo of Portuguese Jewish heritage (the supposed heritage of the forebears of Haym Salomon).

True, there had been an apparent golden age for German Jews, and they had moved in the highest ranks of German life, in government, publishing, industry, and in the German cultural, academic, and scientific worlds. But by 1936 even the German Jews who thought they had given up Judaism were systematically hounded out of the mainstream of German life. This purge was prelude to their physical destruction in Buchenwald, Dachau, and other crematories. The most pronounced German patriotism did not save them, such was the debasement of patriotism under the Nazis.

The progress outside Germany of a people once always persecuted was overshadowed in 1936 by the rise of anti-Semitic Nazism. Against this background of menace and with the hope of preventing further spread of the Nazi cancer, the Patriotic Foundation of Chicago was formed. Its leaders foresaw if but dimly the possibility of a holocaustal tragedy for all the peoples of the world.

It should be stressed that the patriotism of this Foundation was not the overheated or shortsighted pseudo-patriotism of chauvinists. Rather, patriotism was stressed in the positive sense—love for country not hatred for other countrymen, good citizenship rather than a hunt for reasons to discredit those who, to quote Thoreau, marched to a different drumbeat.

Moreover, without any derogation of the role of military figures in the building and preservation of the United States, the Foundation has always endeavored to assure that nonmilitary patriotism would not be overlooked. Enlightened military leaders from George Washington on have acknowledged that military forces would be ineffectual or even unable to function without financial and other assistance from civilians.

Therefore, in its very first announcement the Patriotic Foundation emphasized that people of all races and creeds participated in the upbuilding of America, using Haym Salomon as a symbol of his and other ethnic groups, and also called attention to the indispensable civilian cooperation in the success of the American War of Independence.

Not many monuments, if indeed *any* others, commemorate businessmen of the Revolutionary War. Chicago's memorial helps to compensate for this lack. Both Robert Morris and Haym Salomon represent civilian cooperation in the independence effort—individually and together.

This aspect of the Patriotic Foundation's purpose in sponsoring the monument was clearly delineated in Barnet Hodes' announcement of the formation of the Foundation on July 4, 1936. His statement pointed out that by joining in the work of the Foundation

> leaders in every walk of life, and representatives of every cultural group, have confirmed the conviction that a major contribution to patriotism, historical knowledge, and understanding of the part played by peoples of various nationalities in the building of America will be made by the erection in Chicago of an appropriate memorial symbolizing the cooperation that George Washington received from Robert Morris and Haym Salomon.

It is a matter of history that without the financial genius and support obtained by Robert Morris in conjunction with Haym Salomon ... the armies under Washington would have been seriously handicapped and the prospects of victory in the Revolutionary War dimmed.

The Foundation did not end with the erection of the monument in Heald Square. Although death or retirement has removed some of the original incorporators, Hodes remains active as chairman. He is assisted by, among others, Norman N. Eiger, judge of the Circuit Court of Cook County, who serves as secretary, and a young attorney, Allen H. Dropkin, successor to Laurance H. Armour as treasurer.

Its members feel the Foundation may now be more important than ever. *Civilian* patriotism and *civilian* services to the American nation need to be emphasized and honored because events and trends since the American Revolution, especially since the defeat of Hitler, Mussolini, and Hirohito in World War II, have overemphasized military service. The monument erected in Heald Square offers a lasting kind of balance. So, too, does the continuing program of the Foundation with its message of a national unity which reflects the wholesome pattern of cultural pluralism.

7
Valley Forge

Of all the monuments that punctuate the Chicago scene in parks and along boulevards or on buildings and plazas, from traditional nineteenth-century creations to the modern twentieth-century Picasso on the city's Civic Plaza, none is more meaningful than the monument in Heald Square.

"Men live by symbols." So a much-beloved and very wise American jurist, Supreme Court Justice Oliver Wendell Holmes, once observed. The same may be said of nations, and the monument in Heald Square is a splendid symbol of America. The three figures on its marble plinth together with the bronze liberty tablet and Washington's words carved in stone tell much of the story of how America came into being—and why. The Washington figure alone, in the spiritual courage projected through the sturdy face and steady eyes, in fact the whole frame and stance, particularly symbolizes Valley Forge.

The American Revolution was a long and courage-testing war, a war of not only bloodshed and death and physical bravery but of attrition and endurance. Valley Forge epitomized that endurance.

Indeed, Washington and his troops at Valley Forge represent a most unforgettable stark experience in American history, a deep-etched episode of extreme hardship. This was defiance, in an almost mythological sense, of nature herself for the cause of freedom. Valley Forge does not stand for military activity in the usual sense but for endurance against the lack of food, clothing, medicines, fire wood, and other supplies. Winter at Valley Forge brought misery of heroic dimensions. It tested the manliness of the Continental soldiers, officers and enlisted men, because of the shortage of the most elementary supplies for survival.

Valley Forge exemplified a problem of the American Revolution as a whole. The struggle against British suzerainty and repression continued against a lack of funds for the bare necessities of life. This was true even though France and, to an extent, the Netherlands and Spain eventually arranged for considerable aid to the American cause.

Yale's professor William G. Sumner analyzed the economic situation of the American Revolution:

> The finances of the American Revolution were peculiar from the fact, among others, that they scarcely had a definable base. The regular operations of taxation and public loans did not exist. There was no proper fiscal system for the collection of revenue and disbursement of expenditures. There was only a simulacrum (mere pretense) of a treasury.

The situation, affirmed by modern research, was in fact so desperate that a successful outcome of the struggle was considered impossible without a miracle. (1) A major factor was the great military power of the British Empire, Goliath-like in relation to that of the states in revolt. (2) The Tories remained loyal to the British king. They were the Establishment in many of the cities and towns. (3) A lethargy marked much of the population. It was a deadening kind of neutrality or disinterest. These people were not Tories but nevertheless they were not committed to the cause of freedom. (4) The summertime patriots, of whom Thomas Paine so passionately wrote, included soldiers as well as civilians who let themselves become discouraged as the war dragged on. (5) Jealousies and mistrust existed among the various states. There was a reluctance to establish a unified authority, and the situation was not rectified until the Articles of Confederation were supplanted by the Constitution in 1787.

(6) More frustrating than any other was the problem of supplies, mainly a matter of money. Money for munitions. Money for food. Money for clothing. Money for medicines and other needs of the wounded and sick. Money also for the pittances promised to the soldiers as pay.

Lack of money for the Americans was the British king's "best ally," and this aspect of the revolution was not overlooked by the king and his advisers. As noted by E. P. Oberholtzer, one of Robert Morris' biographers, the king "hoped very confidently that he would gain the victory over his rebellious colonists when they could no longer pay or feed their troops." There were periods when this very situation actually existed.

8
Washington's Money Crisis, 1776-1784

Not only soldiers were plunged into misery by the financial predicament. Civilian leaders of the Revolution, the delegates to the Continental Congress who were the government of the precariously established new nation, were in the grip of the money problem.

Modern America preserves an image of these delegates—the Madisons, Jeffersons, Adamses, Randolphs—as impressive statesmen. They were indeed such, including practically all the signers of the Declaration of Independence, the most prestigious group in American history. But they were also men and were required among other work-a-day things to pay for their board and room. Also, they had family obligations.

As with the soldiers, the delegates were promised compensation, but for long stretches it was not forthcoming. The money simply did not exist. The treasury of the Continental government was usually empty; certainly it was empty of the kind of money acceptable as a medium of exchange for board and room.

Not a few of the delegates faced the most desperate kind of personal financial trouble along with their official financial troubles. "The treasury was so much in arrears to the servants in the public offices," Robert Morris reported in 1781, "that many of them could not, without payment, perform their duties but must have gone to jail for debts they have contracted to enable them to live."

Jefferson also made poignant references to the delegates' plight. He wrote in November 1780 to Benjamin Harrison, then Speaker of the Virginia House of Delegates: "Our Delegates in Congress ... suffer from precarious remittances." On another occasion he noted, "The horses of members of Congress were sometimes turned out into the street because the livery stable keeper was unpaid." James Madison, a principal drafter of the Constitution and later president of the United States, was rescued from his plight by none other than Haym Salomon.

Each of the states that supported the Revolution was supposed to furnish funds for the soldiers and the delegates through appropriations voted by their separate assemblies or conventions. Often the appropriations were not voted or the transmitted funds turned out to be dubious paper notes practically worthless in normal business transactions.

As a result merchants and landlords, even patriotic ones, insisted upon specie or notes backed up by signatures that assured ultimate payment in specie. And specie was scarce—frequently nonexistent—so far as the Treasury of the United States was concerned. Scarce, too, were signatures that made paper acceptable for goods—or so expensive as to be an exploitation of the Revolution for private gain.

For a long period the situation was no better with respect to currency issued by the Continental Congress.

Not even legislation making it a capital crime punishable even by death for refusal to accept Continental currency in payment for supplies for Continental troops changed the situation much.

To make the crisis more desperate the British resorted to a financial trick used by adversaries in other wars, including the United States in World War II. They flooded the countryside with counterfeit Continental notes. This made farmers, merchants, and other suppliers even more wary of accepting any paper unless it was obviously endorsed by someone whose financial standing guaranteed its worth, such as the men on either side of Washington on the Chicago monument.

Oberholtzer observed:

> The currency soon collapsed utterly. It was used to light the fires under offensive Tory gentlemen and to paper the rooms of good Whigs who wished to make an appearance of luxury.... In Philadelphia, men who wore the bills as cockades in their hats marched in a procession through the streets accompanied by a dog which was covered with a coat of tar in which the despised pieces of paper were thickly set. A workman, it was observed, might lose his wages while he was earning them (because of the speed with which the value of the currency kept falling). A merchant's profits were wiped out in a night.... When Congress called for taxes, it was paid in its own money ... which would buy nothing for a suffering army.

Historical materials used in modern histories to document the Revolution devote a great deal of space to the problem of money and the perils resulting from the lack of it. Deserters from the armies included highly patriotic soldiers who could no longer endure actual starvation or insufficient clothing in bitter cold, caused by lack of funds. A whole regiment of soldiers in the Philadelphia line mutinied at one juncture; they had been promised pay, food, clothing, and munitions which never came.

There was the threat, too, of depredation and violence on the part of desperate, angry soldiers. Once Congress had to flee Philadelphia when a company of eighty mutinous soldiers approached to demand money or else. Incidentally, of the government leaders in that particular "time that tried men's souls" only Robert Morris remained in the capital city, and he had to go into hiding.

Some historians argue that there was a certain inevitability about American independence. They cite geographical, political, and emotional reasons as to why the Revolution was bound to succeed. Yet even this view of history would not rule out recognition that whatever was done to lessen the severity of the money problem was a major contribution to the cause. At times the raising of even relatively small sums of money—enough, say, to procure flour for the bread of a regiment for a week, five or six hundred dollars in terms of today's value—took on the proportion of a crucial event.

So the American Revolution was not won easily. It was never a matter of "ten days that shook the world" but a struggle that extended over eight years. Because it was not won easily, it involved much mental and physical suffering. The overriding and continuous question of supplies, of the sinews of war, more than the warring itself accounted for much of that suffering. On the scales the weight of the money problem in terms of mental anguish alone, Washington's in particular, was incalculable.

The proceedings of the Continental Congress, diplomatic correspondence of the period, letters, diaries, and other writings of leading figures of the Revolution are filled with references to financial crisis after financial crisis. It was especially so in the writings of George Washington himself and in those of Thomas Jefferson, James Madison, Benjamin Franklin, John Adams, Edmund Randolph, Gouverneur Morris, Alexander Hamilton, of numerous generals—and, of course, of Robert Morris.

9

Superintendent of Finance

A citizen of Philadelphia, like Haym Salomon, Robert Morris was a businessman-signer of the Declaration of Independence. He also was a member from Pennsylvania of the war-time Continental Congress, the federal government for the colonies in revolt against Great Britain.

In 1781 Morris became superintendent of finance, so he was America's first secretary of the treasury, serving in the most critical financial period in the nation's history.

He confronted the knottiest financial problem ever faced by any secretary of the treasury, for the whole vexing financial situation of the emerging United States was in his lap.

Nor is this the whole story of Robert Morris' function. It is no exaggeration that at crucial times he was all that was important in the civilian government behind Washington's forces. At such times he *was* the civilian government. He thus won the right to be represented for himself and for what he symbolized, standing on a monument alongside Washington, as Lorado Taft saw with an artist's vision.

The commander-in-chief would have approved. In the words of Oberholtzer, "Washington's love for the financier of so many of his campaigns was deep and abiding." The affection was reciprocated by Morris, for Washington was his idol and he would have done anything for him, personally as well as officially.

Not everyone in that time appreciated Washington's virtues, and he had his detractors and conniving rivals. Those who considered Washington as being cold interpreted his strong nature as arrogance.

But Robert Morris and George Washington were two indomitable men who understood each other's strengths and were able to work together effectively. Their country, then and later, benefited. They had first met as fellow delegates to the Continental Congress and were destined to work closely with each other from 1781 on—as closely as they are presented symbolically on the Chicago monument.

Washington was comforted by Morris' taking on the task of ending the financial chaos of the Revolutionary government. He wrote a letter of congratulations on June 4, 1781:

> I felt a most sensible pleasure when I heard of your acceptance of the late appointment of Congress to regulate the finances of this country. My hand and heart shall be with you, and as far as my assistance can go, command it. We have, I am persuaded, but one object in view, the public good, to effect which I will aid your endeavors to the extent of my abilities and with all the powers I am vested with.

For Washington this was an exceptionally warm and personal letter. It was indicative of both Washington's high regard for Robert Morris and his concern over the financial side of the war. Indeed, the financial situation at just this time was in a deepening crisis.

Washington had before him plans for a crucial military campaign. He needed forage, flour, and wagons for an extended march—but he had no acceptable money. In some areas the Army impressed or seized what it wanted, but its agents had to be able to find the needed goods. The harsh truth was that many merchants and farmers, even patriotic ones, hid their goods from the agents. It was "impossible to do business ... without money in hand," the quartermaster general informed the commander-in-chief.

Washington's hope was that Morris would be able to push through a plan for uniform paper money properly secured. He was greatly distressed by the reluctance of the separate states to authorize such currency. "In this, as in most other matters," he commented to William Fitzhugh, "the States individually have acted so independently of each other as to become a mere rope of sand."

For the patriot to develop a workable currency system along with all the other responsibilities of the office of superintendent of finance, no better choice than Robert Morris could have been found. This was true despite attacks made then and later upon Morris, some quite low and insinuating. It was true even though in later life, years after the Revolution had been won, Morris found himself in debtor's prison because of unfortunate over-involvement in the great business fever of the post-Revolutionary period, investment and speculation in western lands.

During the Revolution Robert Morris was granitic strength in the cause of liberty. In its leadership ranks the cause had many philosophers or firebrands such as Thomas Jefferson, James Madison, Sam Adams, Paul Revere, and Thomas Paine, also many hard-headed practical men such as Benjamin Franklin, John Hancock, John Adams, and Alexander Hamilton. But the cause had enlisted few men of outstanding commercial status, who were knowledgeable in large financial and economic dealings from actual involvement over a long period. An obvious reason for the lack was that few such entrepreneurs were in the colonies. Another obvious reason was that the big names in commerce tended to be Tories. Their affluence kept them either loyal to the king or fearful of change.

Morris was unique. He was one of the biggest of big names in business affairs, engaged in importing on a large scale. His interests included building and owning many ships that sailed the seas of the world, and it was commonly understood that he controlled more ships than anyone in America. Later he owned more land than anyone on the continent. He was also engaged in overland transportation, warehousing, and wholesale trade in a vast variety of staple commodities. Inevitably he was involved in loans and credits and he knew the mysteries of banking as did few men in the colonies.

If affluence was supposed to promote loyalty to the king, he had every reason to be a loyalist, but Morris cast his lot with the Revolution. That he did so in the light of his vast interests naturally caused surprise—pained surprise to the Tories but pleasant surprise to the freedom agitators.

Actually, his stand should not have caused surprise. As early as the 1760's he openly opposed the British stamp acts. He was also an early agitator for the non-importation movement even though his own business was adversely affected by the defiant determination of colonials not to buy goods from England until the Crown mended its ways.

It was true—as his enemies never ceased to mention later, embroidering the facts with fictional suspicions— that Morris urged caution. He was not certain that the Declaration of Independence should have been issued when it was, his business sense causing him to advocate further negotiation and a go-slow stance. But when he was outvoted, he went along wholeheartedly and signed his prestigious commercial name to the Declaration with the others who pledged "to each other our Lives, our Fortunes, and our sacred Honor."

Born in England, in Liverpool, he was fourteen when brought to the United States by his father. He recalled England and his youth there with some affection, had numerous English business connections, and was by no means an experimentalist in his views on government. But once he had signed the Declaration, the cause of freedom had no stauncher advocate. Few were more effective in using their expertise where the Revolution was weakest, providing the sinews for the military cutting edges of the cause.

Robert Morris was more representative of the New American—later *the* American type—than Washington. For Washington came from a semi-aristocratic landowning family, destined to be a gentleman. Given other circumstances he very well could have been a king's minister, even a prime minister. He would not have been out of place in the British House of Lords, another Duke of Wellington.

But Morris' father was a nailmaker. It was from ordinary and unprivileged beginnings—like those of his collaborator in Revolutionary War finance, Haym Salomon—that Morris rose to commercial eminence and high governmental office and influence. Like Salomon,

Morris epitomized more than zeal in the American cause of freedom and independence. He also epitomized an important essence of the American dream—ability to rise in the world regardless of heredity, race, or creed. The nailmaker's son became a man of wealth and the nation's chief financial officer, hence the principal in one of America's earliest success stories.

10

"...deserves a great deal of his country"

As superintendent of finance, 1781–1784, Robert Morris was forced to do much more than is suggested by the title of his office.

Morris also directed the marine office, which was the new nation's navy department. In that capacity he supervised the building of ships including privateers and advised as to where and when they would sail. It was he who made possible, for example, the building of a ship for John Paul Jones. He was America's first secretary of the navy as well as its first secretary of the treasury.

The least of his contributions was superintending the allotment of funds that were supposed to come to the Continental treasury through official avenues. He found himself in the position of having to produce the funds when none existed to be supervised.

Only the cause of independence and its ultimate triumph justified the risks that he assumed when engaging in the boldest kind of financing. On one occasion he risked issuing notes against French credits for more than was agreed to by the French king. He hoped the French would not protest the notes, and his bold judgment proved correct. Had it been otherwise, an absolute financial disaster could have engulfed the new nation.

"There is not a single farthing in the military chest," Washington noted gloomily in January 1781, a month before Morris was selected as superintendent of finance and with preparations for the decisive confrontation of Yorktown just ahead. Months passed before the situation was changed much. They were months of reports from Washington and subordinate generals of soldiers starkly hungry and naked or at best clad in makeshift, tattered uniforms, also of mutiny, actual or threatened.

Prodding the various state legislatures to levy, collect, and forward pledged taxes was among Morris' duties. Describing the situation that Morris faced because of the feet-dragging states Washington wrote to a friend, John Armstrong, in March 1781, "States as well as individuals had rather *wish* well than *act* well, had rather *see* a thing done than *do* it." This meant frustration that would have broken a weaker figure, but Morris demonstrated a perseverance in the financial campaign comparable to Washington's in the military campaign.

Morris kept at the states relentlessly and used every kind of appeal, to patriotism, to conscience, and most of all to fear—of defeat, of soldiers going on raids for food, of the armies resorting to impressment of goods. He wrote to the governor of Rhode Island in a typical communication:

> If we will not submit to Great Britain, we must carry on the war, and if we carry on the war, we must have the means. . . . If we cannot get the

means abroad, we must provide them at home; and if we do not provide them by law, they must be taken by force.

Morris raised cash for paying the troops—some payment was vital for their morale—and he also raised cash for the army's commissary agents to purchase supplies. In addition, he took on the tasks of actually providing supplies and arranging for wagons and boats to transport them.

He engaged in the purchase of merchandise not only for the troops but for re-sale, the profits going into the government treasury—one primitive but effective means for raising hard cash.

It is further testimony to Robert Morris' devotion to the cause that, when the Continental treasury was bare at critical times, he used his own funds for purchasing supplies. He placed his personal credit—not infrequently stronger than the government's—behind borrowings for the government and behind debentures issued in the name of the government. He wrote on September 20, 1781, to the Governor of Pennsylvania concerning his exertions for the Yorktown campaign;

> The late movements of the army have so entirely drained me of money that I have been obliged to pledge my personal credit very deeply in a variety of instances, besides borrowing from my friends and advancing . . . every shilling of my own.

A summary by Oberholtzer of the pre-Yorktown requests directed to Morris reveals Washington's reliance on him:

> The Commander-in-Chief . . . made a number of requisitions which *must* be met. It was necessary to place three hundred barrels of flour, the same

quantity of salt meat, and eight or ten hogsheads of rum at the Head of Elk for the subsistence of the troops on their way down to the bay.... Supplies of provisions were needed at other points along the route, and each day while they were marching and during the siege, the men and horses must be fed. Morris also required boats to carry six thousand or seven thousand men.

What Washington requested, Morris somehow supplied. Concerning the requisitions for Yorktown, Morris set down this:

By the greatest exertions, I have at length been able to comply with the General's views, but that compliance has exposed me almost penniless to answer engagements which cannot be violated.

Especially crucial was the support Morris provided permitting Washington to marshal the forces that led to the British surrender at Yorktown in October 1781. That victory, as it turned out, meant that the Revolution had succeeded.

There still remained, however, the need to assure that the effect of Yorktown would not be reversed. Until the peace was signed in 1783 and even later, Morris' services were still needed. To the governor of Maryland Morris forecast the possibility of unpaid angry soldiers pillaging the countryside because they had no choice. He wrote, "Our army, unfed, unpaid, and unclothed, will have to subsist itself, or disband itself.... The States, Sir, *must* give money."

In July 1782 he was told that the state of Virginia intended to meet its obligation but would not do so until the following December. Morris exploded to that state's governor:

What in the name of Heaven can be expected of America but absolute ruin? ... Not until December will Virginia give anything, you say, toward the service of the current year.... How is our country to be defended? How is our army to be supported? Is this what is meant by the solemn declaration to support with life and fortune the independence of the United States?

The annual war budget was about $20,000,000 a year, if the funds were available. For 1782 the states were pledged to contribute at least $8,000,000 as their share of cash outlay, but as of April 1 all that had come in to Morris was $5,500 from one state, New Jersey. It is no wonder that out of desperation he used strong language, the kind that made enemies.

Morris apparently always had detractors, commercial rivals for the most part. He knew that he would make more enemies as a result of the pressures he had to exert as superintendent of finance. After accepting the office Morris noted in his diary:

This appointment was unsought, unsolicited, and dangerous to accept, as it was evidently contrary to my private interests, and, if accepted, must deprive me of those enjoyments, social and domestic, which my time of life required and which my circumstances entitled me to ... and, as a vigorous execution of the duties must inevitably expose me to the resentment of disappointed and designing men, and to the calumny and detraction of the envious and malicious, I was therefore determined not to engage in so arduous an undertaking.

But having accepted the office he promised Washington to do his best to relieve if not solve the financial situation and did pursue a policy of "vigorous execution." As a consequence Morris did not escape the prophesied "calumny," along with the other heartaches and headaches that went with the post.

Once he did think of giving up. Although it was only a threat, Morris advised the Continental Congress in January 1783 that he intended to resign because Congress delayed acting on his proposal for a national tax-gathering agency. Poignant and illuminating correspondence was exchanged with Washington on that occasion:

> I do assure you, Sir, that nothing would have induced me to take this step but a painful conviction that the situation of those to whom the public are indebted is desperate. I believe sincerely that a great majority of the members of Congress wish to do justice; but I as sincerely believe that they will not adopt the necessary measures because they are afraid of offending their states. From my soul, I pity the army and you, my dear Sir, in particular, who must see and feel their distresses without the power of relieving them. . . . I hope my successor will be more fortunate than I have been.

Washington wrote to Morris:

> Very painful sensations are excited in my mind by your letter. It is impossible for me to express to you the regret with which I have received the information it contains. I have often reflected with much solicitude upon the disagreeableness of your situation, and the negligence of the several states in not enabling you to do that justice to the public creditors which your demands require.
>
> I wish the step you have taken may sound the call to their inmost souls and rouse them to a sense

of their own interest, honor, and credit. . . . If your resolutions are absolutely fixed, I assure you I consider the event as one of the most unfortunate that could have fallen upon the states and most sincerely deprecate the sad consequences which I fear will follow.

Alexander Hamilton, later the nation's first official secretary of the treasury by appointment from Washington (a post for which Morris was Washington's first choice), sketched for Washington the desperate situation that confronted Morris:

He had been for some time pressing Congress to obtain funds, and had found a great backwardness in the business. He found the taxes unproductive in the different states; he found the loans in Europe making a very slow progress; he found himself pressed on all hands for supplies; he found himself in short reduced to this alternative, either of making engagements which he could not fulfill, or declaring his resignation in case funds were not established by a given time.

Had he followed the first course, the bubble must soon have burst; he must have sacrificed his credit and his character; and public credit already in a ruinous condition would have lost its last support. He wisely judged it better to resign; this might increase the embarrassment of the moment, but the necessity of the case, it was to be hoped, would produce the proper measures; and he might then resume the direction of the machine with advantage and success. He also had some hope that his resignation would prove a stimulus to Congress.

He was, however, ill-advised in the publication of his letters of resignation. This was an imprudent

step, and has given a handle to his personal enemies, who, by playing upon the passions of others,
have drawn some well-meaning men into the cry
against him. *But Mr. Morris certainly deserves a
great deal of his country. I believe no man in this
country but himself could have kept the money machine agoing during the period he has been in office.* (Italics added.)

The Chicago monument is affirmation of Hamilton's
judgment. Robert Morris, for his service in the cause of
his nation's birth, "certainly deserves a great deal of his
country."

Such also was the judgment of Washington. Modest
about his own great role in the Americans' thrust for
independence, Washington once observed that if any
one individual were to be singled out Robert Morris
"was perhaps most responsible for our success."

The commander-in-chief was thinking of how helpless
he and his Continental armies would have been without
the sinews of war that Morris so effectively helped
provide.

11
Colleagues

To be sure, Morris did not function single-handedly in his service as superintendent of finance. No official could have accomplished what he did without collaboration.

With other businessmen, including Haym Salomon, he brought about the creation of the Bank of North America, in Philadelphia. It served as a national bank, or arm of Morris' office, and helped systematize Morris' operations. In a way that otherwise could not have been achieved the bank's prestige and methods made possible credit arrangements, pyramiding of usable funds, and acceptance of financial paper. The bank also made loans to the Office of Finance though, as one bank director reminded Morris, the loans were most often made on his (Morris') personal credit, not the government's.

Morris had as principal assistant the able Gouverneur Morris, who later participated as a lawyer in the drafting of the Constitution. He was United States minister to France during the French Revolution and afterward United States senator from New York.

To carry out special assignments for him Morris also had the aid of men bearing such familiar English names as John Bradford, Thomas Russell, and John Brown. He worked through a number of brokers but in particular was assisted by the Philadelphian with a different name, Haym Salomon.

In the diary that Morris kept while superintendent of finance (once missing but now on deposit in the Library of Congress) the name Haym Salomon appears about one hundred times from 1781 into 1784, when Morris relinquished his office. Frequently set down by Morris to introduce a record of his day's work was this phrase, "I sent for Haym Salomon."

12
Patriot of the Stock of Abraham

Haym Salomon, who began his American career in New York, was by then a broker in Philadelphia. Broker in that era meant involvement in varied commercial activity. He bought and sold, that is, exchanged at a commission, foreign and domestic currencies, whose values kept fluctuating. He arranged payment for goods bought or sold abroad, acted as agent for sellers or buyers of merchandise, and bought and sold items on his own account.

In modern terms Salomon functioned in an elemental way as if he were a private banker, securities dealer, or member of a commodities exchange. The vital middleman who converted goods into money and guided merchants through the intricacies of foreign exchange and the complexities of the multiple currencies of the separate states was performing an important function in trade.

Salomon operated from a popular Philadelphia establishment called the Coffee House, which served as a kind of general exchange for brokers and merchants. He also used his modest home on Front street between Market and Arch, not far from Robert Morris' headquarters.

Robert Morris undoubtedly knew about him, may even have had private dealings with him before their official relationship developed. Being a frequent advertiser in the Philadelphia newspapers Salomon was already well known. One of his advertisements appeared in the Pennsylvania Journal February 28, 1781:

A Few Bills of Exchange on
France, St. Eustatia & Amsterdam
To be Sold by
Haym Salomon, Broker

The said Salomon will attend every day at the COFFEE HOUSE between the hours of twelve and two, where he may be met with, and any kind of business in the brokering way, will be undertaken by him; and those Gentlemen who chuse to favour him with this business may depend on the greatest care and punctuality.

The statement by George Washington in 1790 that contained these ringing words, "the Government of the United States . . . gives to bigotry no sanction, to persecution no assistance," was addressed to the Jewish community of Newport, Rhode Island. It also contained a statement with an interesting biblical style:

May the children of the stock of Abraham who dwell in this land continue to merit and enjoy the good will of the other inhabitants—while everyone shall sit in safety under his own fig tree and there shall be none to make him afraid.

Haym Salomon was a member of the stock of Abraham referred to by Washington in his message. He was one of the early Jewish immigrants, of whom there were more in America around the time of the Revolution than is usually thought. In the various colonies, North and South, were probably three thousand Jews at the time of the Declaration of Independence. Some had arrived as early as 1654.

"It is thus a noteworthy fact, of interest to all Americans," observed Nathan M. Pusey, president of Harvard University, in a 1954 address commemorating the 300th anniversary of Jewish participation in the settlement of America, "that almost from the beginning Jewish families were actively contributing to the new pattern of life being built on this continent."

"How came they here?" the poet Henry Wadsworth Longfellow asked in his tribute, *In the Jewish Cemetery at Newport*.

The answer, of course, is that they came in the same pattern of movement to the new continent as did the Puritans and the Quakers and similar religious groups, all persecuted or held down in one way or another in their countries of origin and all hoping for a better life generally. They came for the opportunities of a new land. They came for an end to Old World handicaps imposed on people of ordinary status, not on the nobility or other privileged classes. They came for freedom from Old World religious persecutions and restrictions.

To be sure, some newcomers migrated solely for economic reasons, which included escape from disastrous local conditions abroad unrelated to persecution—famine, unemployment, and the like. But the motivation of freedom was clearly the most substantial factor of the American dream—out of which came the American Revolution and the American institutions that followed it.

In the Old World the Jews were ever conscious of the

threat of persecution even in times or areas of quiet and tolerance, and they naturally shared this dream of freedom in America and desired to give reality to it. With very few exceptions the Jews in America during the Revolutionary period were patriots, activists in or sympathetic adherents to the cause of independence. A sizable percentage served in the Continental armies.

Haym Salomon was definitely one of the patriots. He was imprisoned by British military authorities in New York on the charge of subversive activity, in his words "taken up as a spy," an active partisan of the Revolution perhaps as a member of the underground Sons of Liberty.

It is necessary to say "perhaps" because there is no written register for the Sons of Liberty. It was a secret group, vague and shadow-like for obvious reasons. Membership was mainly by deed rather than by formality.

A few patriots such as Alexander McDougall of New York, later a general in the war, were known openly as Sons of Liberty, but most were anonymous. They were considered Sons of Liberty because they could be depended upon for service in the cause even in areas still held by the British, such as New York as in Salomon's case.

The understanding among Haym Salomon's descendants that he was a Son of Liberty and that the British acted on the same understanding may not be documented, but his having been imprisoned by the British as a spy for the American cause is a matter of record. Long before his association with Robert Morris as a businessman in the financing of the patriotic cause, Haym Salomon had made clear where he stood and had suffered for that stand.

Many patriots, not excepting Washington himself, have been the targets of amateur and professional history students, whose motives are presented as objective but are mainly cynical or in the service of some purpose other than historical. Washington Irving once commented about such history-workers:

> There is a certain meddlesome spirit which, in the garb of learned research, goes prying about the traces of history, casting down its monuments, and marring and mutilating its fairest trophies. Care should be taken to vindicate great names from such pernicious erudition.

Haym Salomon's right to be called a patriot has been slurred even by co-religionists. True, some claims made years back for him have to be reassessed, and no complaint is made against factual research that leads to proper reassessment. But sweeping rejection of Salomon's role in the Revolution cannot be supported. His right to honor from Americans is undeniably fact-based, as solid as the base of the monument on which he stands with Washington and Morris.

13

Earlier Service in the Cause

Salomon was born in Poland about 1740 in the province of Poznan in Western Poland. At that time the town was called Leszno and remained so named until 1772, when Poland went through one of its partitions between Prussia and Russia. The town became part of Prussia or Germany and was called Lissa. That year is when Haym Salomon, then in his early thirties, is understood to have left Leszno or Lissa permanently.

Since 1919 it is again called Leszno, its Polish name, after the family of Leszczynski, of which King Stanislaw I was a member. It is also the birthplace of Leo Baeck, who was Chief Rabbi of Berlin during the Hitler period in Germany.

A spirit of freedom pervaded this Polish town in Haym Salomon's youth when it was deeply involved in the Reformation agitation and became a stronghold of the Moravians, who established offshoots early in America. Apparently there existed also some unpleasant religious currents for a Jewish lad, strong pressures for conversion that were resisted by Haym and his family.

This self-reliant youth with exceptional interest in the world outside the close-knit, tradition-steeped Jewish community in Leszno may have engaged in "travels" (his word) even before leaving Poland permanently. That would explain why he already spoke or was familiar with not only English but several other languages when he appeared in New York. The ability stood him in good stead, perhaps even saving his life, at the time of his imprisonment by the British; it was also a critical factor in his services in the Revolutionary cause.

The other languages included German, French, Russian, Italian, and probably Dutch—a remarkable achievement for a man of little formal education. His education in languages as well as in commerce and finance came from his travels. Interesting documentation on this is among Salomon data in the archives of the American Jewish Historical Society. Salomon wrote a business associate and friend, Isaac Myers of New York, in April 1783. He communicated through him with his father back in Poland because he could not write though he could speak the one language his father used, Yiddish.

Please to mention to my father the difficulties that I have labored under in not having any learning, and that I should not have known what to have done had not it been for the languages that I learned in my travels, such as French, English, etc.

Therefore I would advise him and all my relatives to have their children well educated, particularly in the Christian languages and, should any of my brothers' children have a good head to learn Hebrew, I would contribute toward their being instructed.

The father's name was Solomon or Salomon (as Haym's name was variously spelled in various documents), which was the father's only name after the biblical custom which prevailed then in the Old World among Jewish families. A letter to Europe signed "Haim son of Reb Solomon" (*Reb* standing for *Mr.*) reveals how the son obtained his family name.

The parents apparently were always quite poor, and in his rise to relative affluence Haym, the immigrant from Lissa, like Robert Morris, the immigrant from Liverpool, was an example of the success story that America represents for many immigrants.

By some accounts Salomon came to America and New York in 1772, by others in 1775. His own statement bearing on this point is in a memorial to Congress mentioning that he was in New York "some time before the Entry of the British Troops at said City of New York" in 1776. In that period he was not yet a broker but a sutler, that is, a purveyor of goods to soldiers, both Continental troops and British troops, which placed him in a good position to function as a spy for the Americans.

He was watched carefully by both sides, but his sympathies were clearly with the colonies. A document among the papers of the American general Philip Schuyler in the New York Public Library collection affirms that "Haym Salomon, sutler," was to be trusted by Continental forces and permitted to be within Continental lines.

His marriage on January 2, 1777, to Rachel Franks, then only fifteen, gave Salomon some in-laws who were well established in both New York and Philadelphia. Her father was Moses Benjamin Franks, a Philadelphia merchant, and her brother, Isaac Franks, served in the war as an officer on Washington's staff.

These connections, perhaps with a dowry, may have enhanced his business status. In 1778, according to advertisements in the New York Gazette and Weekly Advertiser, he was the proprietor of a store in New York City, first at 222 Broad street, "near the Post Office," and then at 245 Broad street, "near the City Hall." He specialized in provisions for ships, his announcements stating, "Captains of ships and others can depend upon being supplied on most reasonable terms."

He prospered. In July 1778 his wife gave birth to a boy, who was named Ezekiel. Then the British military authorities struck at him as one who was a sympathizer and more with the American cause while remaining in British-occupied New York. He estimated that at the time of his arrest he was worth "to the amount of five or six thousand Pounds sterling."

The prison in which he was held, called the Provost, was an ill-equipped, hated, disease-breeding, tomb-like place. But the British either were not too sure of a case against him or desperately needed someone to communicate in German with their Hessian troops; Salomon was made a trustee, placed on probation, even permitted to continue in business so long as he helped with the Hessians.

Salomon's unusual prisoner status enabled him to help the American cause even more. In collaboration with a French prisoner, Samuel Demezes, he urged the Hessians to desert and backed his verbal persuasion with money to help them escape behind American lines. The exploit was as risky as it was incredible.

The British discovered what he was doing. Ahead of another arrest which this time might have meant his death, he fled to Philadelphia, forced to leave wife and baby behind. *Papers of the Continental Congress, no. 41, fol. 58*, as noted in *Journal of the Continental Congress 11* (1778): page 840 includes a poignant communication in which Salomon gives the basic facts about this episode:

To the Honorable the Continental Congress:
The memorial of Haym Salomon late of the City of
New York, Merchant. Humbly Sheweth.

That your Memorialist was some time before the
Entry of the British Troops at the said City of New
York and soon taken up as a spy and by General
Robertson committed to the Provost—That by the
Interposition of Liet. General Heister (who wanted
him on account of his knowledge in the French,
Polish, Russian, Italian etc. Languages) he was
given over to the Hessian Commander who appointed him in the Commissary Way as purveyor
chiefly for the Officers—That being at New York he
has been of great service to the French and American prisoners and has assisted them with Money
and helped them off to make their Escape—That
this and his close connexions with such of the Hessian Officers as were inclined to resign, and with
Monsieur Samuel Demezes, has rendered him at
last so obnoxious to the British Head Quarters that
he was already pursued by the Guards and on Tues-
day the 11th inst, he made his happy Escape from
thence—This Monsieur Demezes is now most bar-
barously treated at the Provost's and is seemingly
in danger of his life. And the Memorialist begs
leave to cause him to be remembered to Congress
for an Exchange.

Your memorialist has upon this Event most ir-
revocably lost all his Effects and Credits to the
amount of five or six thousand Pounds sterling and
left his distressed Wife and a Child of a Month Old
at New York waiting that they may soon have an
opportunity to come out from thence with empty
hands.

In these Circumstances he most humbly prayeth
to grant him any Employ in the way of his Busi-

ness whereby he may be enabled to support himself and family.—And your Memorialist is in duty bound etc. etc.

Haym Salomon

Phila. Aug. 25, 1778

There is no record that the Continental Congress did more than send Salomon's memorial to the Board of War or that the Board of War did anything for him. Congress and the Board obviously faced bigger problems than the plight of the new Philadelphian.

His memorial is a record set down at the time, not a recollection, that documents the point already mentioned. Even before his collaboration in financial matters with Robert Morris, Salomon had served the American cause at great risk to his life and fortune. And he wished to be of further service in the cause.

14

"Usefull to the Public Interest"

By the time Robert Morris first sent for him in 1781, Salomon had reestablished himself in business in Philadelphia, as a broker. He was already serving the patriot cause as the banker for France, America's principal ally. When French forces began arriving in America, French bills of exchange had to be converted into American currency for purchasing supplies and also for disbursing pay to French soldiers and sailors. Salomon was selected by the French king's minister to the United States, the Chevalier de la Luzerne, to handle the operations, and he did so without charge.

Published records of French assistance to the American Revolution are far from complete, causing some cynical historians to question Haym Salomon's connection with the French government despite his own *contemporary* references. However, cynicism is unwarranted. In 1938 the French ambassador to the United States, Doynel de Saint-Quentin, ordered a study of the

French archives for Salomon's role at the request of Chairman Hodes of the Patriotic Foundation. On October 25 the Ambassador sent the following communication:

*Ambassade
de la République Française
aux Etats-Unis.*

Washington, le   October 25th, 1938.

My dear Mr. Hodes,

It is with gratification that I learned that the Patriotic Foundation of Chicago intends to erect in Chicago a monument commemorating the friendship which existed between George Washington, Robert Morris and Haym Solomon. The last named has indeed special claims to the gratitude of the French nation. We have not forgotten that during the days of the American Revolution Mr. Solomon acted as General Paymaster of the French Expeditionary Corps and performed this difficult task with a high degree of proficiency.

I wish full success to your project which will recall one of the glorious epochs of the amity between the French and American peoples./.

Believe me, my dear Mr. Hodes,

Yours very sincerely,

Mr. Barnet Hodes,
  Corporation Counsel,
    City of Chicago -Law Department,
      Chicago,
        Ill.

France was not the only ally served by Salomon in the cause of the Revolution. When Dutch interests, "merchants of the United Provinces," as he described them, made loans to the American government, he handled the conversion of the Dutch paper also. The Spanish ambassador to the United States, through whom secret assistance to the cause was rendered by Spain, likewise depended upon Salomon for financial service.

When money from Spain failed to get through the British blockade, Salomon with his personal funds supported the Spanish ambassador, Don Francisco Rendon, in Philadelphia. It was important for American morale that Spain appear to be an active friend, and Salomon's temporary support of Rendon was vital. A record of this help is in a letter written in 1783 by Rendon to the Spanish governor of Cuba, Don José Marie de Navarro:

> Mr. Salomon has advanced the money for the service of his most Catholic Majesty and I am indebted to his friendship, in this particular, for the support of my character as his most Catholic Majesty's agent here, with any degree of credit and reputation.

It was, however, Salomon's service to the French forces that induced Robert Morris to begin their close relationship. On June 8, 1781, Morris wrote in his diary:

> I agreed with Mr. Haym Salomon the Broker, who has been employed by Officers of His Most Chris'n Majesty to make Sale of their Army and Navy Bills, to assist me.

Morris' office was then receiving French bills directly. Various observations in his diary indicate that Morris was not satisfied with other brokers, who were charging commissions up to five percent and higher. Salomon desired to serve the cause and made plain that he would never charge more than one-fourth of one percent, half his normal rate for private clients. As much as the moderate charges Morris appreciated Salomon's exceptional expertise and connections abroad and at home along with his patriotic zeal.

Was Washington aware of Salomon's services? It is reasonable to assume that he was, for Morris' diary reveals Washington came often to Morris' office in 1782 and 1783 to discuss financial matters, and it was then that Salomon was notably active in his collaboration with Morris.

The following random entries in Morris' diary are evidence of Salomon's close association:

May 8 [1782]. I sent for Mr. Haym Salomon.

June 25. Mr. Haym Salomon came to inform me that he can buy Bills.

July 1st. Haym Salomon the Broker informs me that he is applied to by Sundry Persons to sell Bills. I desired him to procure me Customers.

July 10. Haym Salomon came respecting Bills.

August 27. I sent for Salomon.

August 28. Salomon the Broker came and I urged him to leave no stone unturned to find out Money—or the means by which I can obtain it.

Jan. 16 [1783]. Mr. Haym Salomon respecting Bills of Exchange. I consulted him about raising the price, he advises me to secure a good deal of Money first as he thinks an attempt to raise the Price will stop the Sale for some time and I am of the same opinion.

In Morris' letterbooks are copies of correspondence revealing as to the relationship. For example:

Office of Finance 8th
April 1782

Mr. Haym Salomon,
Sir,

You are to deliver unto Michael Hillegas Esqr Treasurer of the United States all the Notes which you have received from the Persons to whom you sold the Bills No. 1 to 42 amounting to Lvr 500,000. sold for 34.758"18–2. Pennsylvania Currency agreeable to the List of said Notes annexed hereto, you are to receive in Return Mr. Hillegas's duplicate Receipts specifying the Notes and Sums one of which receipts upon being produced to and deposited with Joseph Nourse Esqr Register of the Treasury will acquit you of this Claim, the other you may keep for your own Satisfaction and Security. You will render a separate Account of your Brokerage to Mr. Milligan the Comptroller and on his Certificate I will grant you a Warrant for the Amount.
I am Sir

Your humble Servant
RM

After the war was over, Salomon placed in the Pennsylvania Journal and Weekly Advertiser for January 1, 1785, the following about his extensive service for Morris on foreign subsidies:

By being Broker to the Office of Finance, and honored with its confidence, all those sums have passed through his hands, which the generosity of the French Monarch, and the affection of the merchants of the United Provinces, prompted them to furnish us with, to enable us to support the expense of the war, and which have so much contributed to its successful and happy termination.

Salomon risked his own funds and credit behind French paper, as indicated by a notice he published in the Independent Gazette of Philadelphia for April 19, 1783:

HAYM SALOMON

Takes this method of acquaint all those who possess full Sets of Bills of Exchange, drawn in his favor and endorsed by him on Monsieur Boutin, Treasurer of the Marine Department of France, that they shall, on application, have the money refunded; and for bills of the above description which may have already been sent to France, satisfactory assurance will be given to the proprietors that they shall be paid, agreeable to their relative tenors, in Paris, April 19.

An important service was handling sales of French bills to maintain the market for them. Any decline was costly to the American treasury, and it became a passion with Salomon to maintain the prices of the bills he helped to sell. On August 9, 1781, Gouveneur Morris wrote of Salomon:

He informs me of Sundry Persons selling French Bills. I desire him to gain Information of the Persons, the Sums, the Rates, to call on them and urge them to keep up the Price, to threaten them, to give me intelligence tomorrow morning.

It is no wonder that when he asked of Robert Morris a personal favor, permission to state in his advertisements that he was "Broker to the Office of Finance,"

67

Robert Morris took time to comment in his diary in July 1782:

> This broker has been *usefull to the public interest* (italics added) and requests leave to publish himself as broker to the office, to which I have consented, as I do not see any disadvantage can possibly arise to the public service but the reverse, and he expects individual benefits therefrom.

Typical advertising, including the frequently misspelled name, is the following from the Freeman's Journal of Philadelphia for November 6, 1782:

HAYM SOLOMONS,

Broker to the Office of Finance, to the Consul General of France, and to the Treasurer of the French Army,

At his office in Front street, between Market & Arch streets.

Buys and sells on commission Bank Stock, Bills of Exchange on France, Spain, Holland, and other parts of Europe, the West Indies, and inland bills, at the usual commissions.

He buys & sells Loan Office Certificates, Continental and State Money, of this or any other state, paymaster and quartermaster general's notes; these, and every other kind of paper transactions (bills of exchange excepted) he will charge his employers no more than One Half Per Cent for his commission.

He procures Money on Loan for a short time and gets notes and bills discounted.

Gentlemen and others residing in this state, or any of the United States, by sending their orders to the office, may depend on having their business transacted with as much fidelity and expedition as if they were themselves present.

He receives tobacco, sugars, tea, and every other sort of goods, to sell on commission, for which purpose he has provided proper stores.

He flatters himself, his assiduity, punctuality, and extensive connections in his business, as a broker, is well established in various parts of Europe, and in the United States in particular.

All persons who shall please to favour him with their business, may depend upon his utmost exertion for their interest, and part of the Money Advanced if desired.

"Usefull to the public interest." Those words by Robert Morris, not a man to pay compliments idly, sum up Haym Salomon's official service. They affirm the recognition that Salomon receives personally and symbolically on the Chicago monument—this recognition supported by Albert Bushnell Hart, Harvard University professor of history, who wrote:

All Americans of all races may acclaim Haym Salomon as a patriot, a benefactor to his country, an inciter of patriotism . . . to his countrymen of all races and to later generations.

15
Private Benefactor

Salomon was also a man of private benefactions. Most laudable was his assistance to members of the Continental Congress who found themselves without funds.

As noted earlier one of those whom he helped was James Madison of Virginia, a principal drafter of the Constitution and a two-term president of the United States. In one letter to Edmund Randolph on August 27, 1782, Madison told of his financial predicament and how Haym Salomon, whose "pensioner" he was, bailed him out. Another letter on September 30, in *The Writings of James Madison*, edited by Gaillard Hunt (1900), elaborated on Salomon's help:

> I am almost ashamed to reiterate my wants so incessantly to you, but they begin to be so urgent that it is impossible to suppress them. The kindness of our little friend in Front street, near the coffee-house, is a fund which will preserve me from extremities, but I never resort to it without great

mortification, as he obstinately rejects all recompense. The price of money is so usurious, that he thinks it ought to be extorted from none but those who aim at profitable speculations. To a necessitous Delegate he gratuitously spares a supply out of his private stock.

Madison was not the only delegate to Congress who was generously helped by Salomon to stay on the job in Philadelphia. Thomas Jefferson, Arthur Lee, Joseph Jones, and James Wilson were also tided over by funds from Salomon's "private stock." The advances were not only interest free but made in the knowledge that repayment would be a long time coming if at all. As Gouveneur Morris observed about the plight of those delegates, "The person who did loan anything to a member to relieve his distress in that day was in no expectation of ever getting repaid."

Salomon similarly aided a number of army officers. Like the delegates to Congress they were in financial distress because of the lack of government funds. General Mifflin, General St. Clair, Colonel Morgan, Major McPherson, and General von Steuben were among such beneficiaries. There is evidence, too, that funds advanced by Salomon kept entire volunteer soldier groups from disbanding.

These sums were small in relation to the funds that passed through Salomon's hands in the Office of Finance, but they tell a good deal about Salomon, the patriot-businessman. Many years later in 1830 a son of Salomon's sent Madison, then in retirement, some papers bearing Madison's and others' names, papers that concerned the advances. He asked Madison what the papers meant. Madison did indeed recall the help from Haym Salomon for himself and other members of the Continental Congress. He commented:

The transactions shown by the papers you enclosed were the means of effectuating remittances for the support of the delegates, and the agency of your father therein was solicited on account of the respectability and confidence he enjoyed among those best acquainted with him.

Along with his business activity Salomon was a man who accepted responsibility in civic affairs, in his religious community, and in his family relationships.

As were both Washington and Morris, he was a Mason. When funds were needed for the poor in Philadelphia, he was a leading contributor. He collaborated with other businessmen for advancing the city's position as a commercial and political center. When Congress moved from Philadelphia to Princeton in 1783 causing dismay to the business community, Salomon was among the signers of a call (drafted by Thomas Paine) that urged Congress not to abandon Philadelphia.

The historic Jewish congregation in Philadelphia, Mikveh Israel, had his active support, and he was a member of its governing board. When the congregation built its first synàgogue, Salomon alone contributed one-fourth of the cost.

His allegiance to the Jewish community was put to a test in 1783. The Pennsylvania Frame of Government or constitution included a provision that, in effect, barred Jews from being members of the state legislature. It required that before being seated legislators must "acknowledge the Scriptures of the Old and New Testament to be given by Divine Inspiration." This was a controversial matter that a businessman might wish to avoid. But Salomon joined in signing a petition from the Jewish community to the Pennsylvania Board of Censors, whose concerns included civil rights, asking that the provision be removed. It was removed when

Pennsylvania adopted a new constitution—an early landmark in the story of American civil liberties.

Salomon did not forget his parents in Poland although during the Revolutionary War, when ship movements were restricted, he apparently had no correspondence with them. In what turned out to be one of his last years though he was still in his forties, he wrote to a cousin in Charleston, South Carolina, on June 20, 1783, of

> the Joy I feel in hearing from my parents after so long an absence, a Joy more easily conceived than expressed, and in relieving them in their indigent Circumstances which, by God's blessing, I hope to enable them to live above want for the future.

He began sending money to his parents and sent a gold chain to his mother.

Word spread in the town of his birth that he was an exceedingly wealthy man in America. An uncle, then in England, wrote to ask that Salomon set up "yearly allowances" for relatives in Poland and also requested that one of his sons be invited to live with Salomon. He sent the uncle some money but politely and firmly corrected his relative's notions about his wealth in a letter dated July 10, 1783:

> Your ideas of my riches are too extensive. Rich I am not, but the little I have I think it my duty to share with my poor father and mother. They are the first that are to be provided for by me, and must and shall have the preference.
>
> Whatever little more I can squeeze out, I will give my relations, but I tell you plainly and truly that it is not in my power to give you or any relations yearly allowances. Don't you nor any of them expect it. Don't fill your mind with vain and idle

73

expectations and golden dreams that never will nor can be accomplished. Besides my father and mother, my wife and children must be provided for. I have three young children, and as my wife is very young may have more, and if you and the rest of my relations will consider these things with reason, they will be sensible of this I now write. But notwithstanding this I mean to assist my relations as far as it lays in my power.

In thus fending off the notion of the uncle that he was a man of great wealth Salomon described his position more accurately than perhaps even he realized. The securities in his personal portfolio, which included Continental currency, treasury certificates, and various state certificates, in face value totalled $353,729.33. When those securities were liquidated after his death, they brought in only $44,732 against debts of $45,292. The end result was that his wife and children—by then there were four including a son Haym M. only three weeks old—were left with practically nothing.

Salomon had been planning to launch a business on Wall street in New York in partnership with Jacob Mordecai, but he was ailing in health for some time and died while still in Philadelphia on January 6, 1785. The *Pennsylvania Packet* of Philadelphia carried in its issue of January 11 a notice of the end of his career at age 45:

Thursday last, expired, after a lingering illness, Mr. Haym Salomons, an eminent broker of this city; he was a native of Poland, and of the Hebrew nation. He was remarkable for his skill and integrity in his profession, and for his generous and human deportment. His remains were on Friday last deposited in the burial ground of the synagogue, in this city.

16
Controversy

Controversy about Salomon was later stirred over the nature of the securities in his portfolio. Did they represent security for loans that Salomon made to or for the Continental government out of his personal funds? If so, was the government honorbound to reimburse the estate and heirs of Haym Salomon?

His younger son, Haym M., prepared a case in the affirmative and pressed it upon Congress from the 1840's to the 1860's. He presented a case so strong that nine out of ten Congressional committees that studied it over the years issued reports endorsing the claim. One recommended as reimbursement a grant of land, another suggested a gold medal to commemorate Salomon's services. Congress as a whole did not act. Absolute, affirmative documentation on the meaning of the securities was not possible; there was an understandable reluctance to set a precedent for a claim going so far back in time; and some descendants of Salomon asked that the matter be dropped. The matter is important now only as a postscript for the record. Motivation and purpose for the Chicago monument had nothing to do with the claim.

Also part of the record is a movement begun in the 1920's by the Federation of Polish Jews in America to erect a statue of Haym Salomon in New York City. The controversy became so heated that the project had to be dropped. Opposition was expressed on the premise that Salomon's personal financial assistance to the government was exaggerated in the publicity material announcing the proposed statue, and the project became involved in debate related to the claims made by Salomon's son. It was *not* disputed, however, that Salomon was a patriot during the Revolution, a man who served the cause of independence.

Because Salomon is one of its three figures, the Chicago monument did not escape echoes of the New York controversy. However, the Chicago project went forward to fruition because it was not a monument to individuals but represented two important concepts: (1) civilian cooperation with the military was a vital factor in the winning of independence, and (2) people of all creeds and origins participated from the beginning in the upbuilding of the nation.

Salomon, a civilian and a Polish Jewish immigrant, symbolizes both concepts when standing with Washington and Morris.

The whole subject of Salomon and the Chicago monument was reviewed by the distinguished historian, Dr. Jacob Rader Marcus, Adolph S. Ochs Professor of Jewish History at Hebrew Union College, Jewish Institute of Religion, and director of the American Jewish Archives, Cincinnati. In *Early American Jewry*, II, (1953) Dr. Marcus wrote:

If it is understood that Salomon is a symbol of the participation of the American Jew in the struggle for independence, then he merits the memorial. The American Revolution was a 'Battle of the Nations' for freedom: English, Scots, Irish, Germans, Dutch, and a host of others . . . the 'huddled masses yearning to breathe free, the wretched refuse . . . the homeless, tempest-tossed.' All these groups helped build America.

He was Colonial America at its best. As a symbol and as a man he merits not only the respect and affection of this generation, but also the monument which his admirers built to do him honor.

17

The Monument Conceived

The beginning of an important project is always interesting. So it was with the Patriotic Foundation of Chicago and its project to win historical recognition for Haym Salomon and Robert Morris. Both the original and present memberships comprise persons of various faiths and walks of life, a cross section of American society.

Although the concept originated with one individual, Barnet Hodes, now senior member of a prominent Chicago law firm, the foundation is not a one-man affair. Many well-known Chicagoans have been associated with it and its goals.

Hodes is of Polish Jewish heritage, so it was natural for him to become interested in Haym Salomon's career. He grew up in Illinois, in the small city of LaSalle, the only Jewish lad in his high school classes, keenly interested in American history and keenly proud of being an American.

He was puzzled that history books, encyclopedias, school textbooks, and the like seldom mentioned contributions by Jews in the founding and development of America. There were frequent mentions of Von Steuben, the German; of Pulaski and Kosciusko, Poles; of MacDougall, the Scot; of Carroll, Roman Catholic; of Penn, the Quaker; and of figures with names suggesting Protestant Anglican origin.

But what about American Jews? Searching in the meagre library materials of his town he found nothing until one day he came upon the writings of Madison C. Peters. In them and along research trails that Peters' pioneer work opened up he discovered numerous Jews who had been soldiers in the American Revolution—Frank, Sheftall, Mordecai, Cohen, Joseph, among others. He learned that the entire Jewish congregation of New York City under Rabbi Gerson Seixas had moved at great sacrifice from New York to Philadelphia rather than remain after New York was captured by the British. He also learned about Haym Salomon.

During his senior year at high school he entered a state-wide oratorical contest. Fired by his discoveries about his compatriots he titled his speech, *Is the Jew a Patriot?* and included much about Haym Salomon. He won the contest.

From that time on Hodes was subject to a fixed idea, some day he would see that the services of Haym Salomon symbolizing Jewish participation in the American Revolution were properly commemorated and that the neglect of Jews in history texts would be corrected.

By 1935 Hodes had a more mature view. A monument to Haym Salomon alone or to any other single Jewish figure in America's beginnings would not express what he felt was desirable. Needed was a monument that would dramatize an America made up of and made by people of *various* origins. Haym Salomon would symbolize that fact only if he were grouped with non-Jewish figures. The emphasis should be not on individuals but on their collaboration—Christians and Jews, civilians and military men.

Washington was the natural and inevitable symbol of military contribution to the Revolution; Robert Morris symbolized civilian support for the military, so did Haym Salomon because of his association with Morris as well as his earlier patriotism.

By now Hodes, still in his thirties, occupied a position of prestige in Chicago. He had been a member of the City Council and also of the Illinois State Commission. That year he was appointed Corporation Counsel of Chicago, chief legal officer of the municipal corporation. Also in 1935 he was chosen by the Junior Association of Commerce as "outstanding young Chicagoan of the year" for his reorganization of the city's law department into a model for the cities of the nation. He was founding head of the National Municipal Law Officers Association, sister group of the Conference of United States Mayors.

All his influence was placed behind a movement to organize the Patriotic Foundation of Chicago. Its first step would be a monument to express the concept of America's cultural pluralism in contrast to the racism festering in Europe under the Nazis of Germany.

Much faster than such groups are usually formed, Hodes had a list of one hundred Chicagoans as members of a sponsoring group. They represented all elements, industry and labor, professions, the academic world, veterans' groups, major political parties, and all faiths, including ministers, rabbis, and priests as well as prominent religious laymen. Though still in the idea stage, the project had been born.

In the meantime Hodes communicated to the venerable sculptor, Lorado Taft, his zeal for the project. The two were brought together in cordial association by Taft's son-in-law, Professor Paul H. Douglas of the University of Chicago, who later became a United States senator from Illinois.

Then in his seventies Taft was still active in the artistic career he had begun fifty years before. Among his achievements were the *Fountain of Time* facing Chicago's Midway; Blackhawk, the Indian chief, overlooking the Rock River near Oregon, Illinois; the Columbus memorial fountain in Washington, D.C.; and Abraham Lincoln at Urbana, Illinois.

Himself a descendant of Revolutionary War patriots, Taft became enthusiastic. The monument's purpose, he told Hodes, coincided with his own views on the meaning of America. This was an important endorsement from an eminent artist and an eminent American citizen.

The foundation later showed its appreciation for Taft's collaboration:

> It is indeed fitting that the execution of this memorial to Washington, Morris, and Salomon, sponsored by Chicagoans and intended for Chicago, should be entrusted to the master hands of Chicago's own internationally famous sculptor.... Certainly no artist more able than this beloved genius could have been found for such an important assignment.

Even before he was formally commissioned, Taft put aside other work to create a model which forecast in miniature the more than life-size standing bronze figures on a mammoth base of rectangular marble. It was all the more effective for being a concept of simplicity. The model permitted visual presentations, and the result was a kind of magic that lifted the project from idea to near reality.

When a public announcement was made on Independence day 1936 that the Patriotic Foundation of Chicago had been formed, it was also announced that Taft would be the artist and designer of the monument. He wrote to Hodes from his Midway Studios in August, "I am waiting eagerly for the word 'go' and shall do my best on the fine subject which you have given me." But the word go had to wait for funds to be raised.

The then mayor of Chicago, Roman Catholic Edward J. Kelly, was honorary chairman. Two co-chairmen were Barnet Hodes and Colonel A. A. Sprague, well-known Protestant civic leader. Edgar L. Schnadig, prominent businessman, served as executive vice-chairman, Laurance H. Armour, banker member of the meat-packing family, as treasurer, and Judge Norman N. Eiger, then an assistant corporation counsel, as secretary who helped coordinate a staff of publicists and researchers. There were notable additions to the group

Lorado Taft, a great American, a great sculptor, is shown as he finished model for monument.

82

of representative Chicagoans earlier enlisted: Governor of Illinois Henry Horner, United States Judge Otto Kerner, advertising-world figure A. D. Lasker, University of Chicago historian William E. Dodd, then United States Ambassador to Germany, Harris Perlstein, well known civic leader, among others.

To defray the monument's cost of $50,000 there were several choices. The sum could be contributed by a few well-to-do individuals or one wealthy person or a foundation. Several men on the executive-advisory committee were wealthy enough and interested enough to underwrite the entire cost of the monument. These possibilities were vetoed on the principle that a symbol of democracy should be paid for democratically. At the outset the Foundation said:

> To make possible this inspiring monument is a task in which all may and should have a part. It would be contrary to the spirit of the movement if this were not so—if merely a small group of individuals were responsible for it. It is and should be an all-Chicago contribution.

A hard path was chosen because the United States had not yet recovered from the great Depression. At times Hodes and his associates felt as Robert Morris and Haym Salomon must have felt about the difficulties of raising money, even for a good cause. But a persistent campaign was kept up.

18
Widespread Support

Help came from many prominent Americans. President Franklin D. Roosevelt's endorsement of the monument topped a large stack of impressive statements.

"I am indeed gratified to learn that belated recognition is to be made of the invaluable services rendered to the cause of the American Revolution by Haym Salomon," Roosevelt wrote to Hodes from the White House on August 24, 1936. "The debt of gratitude which the Nation owes Salomon's memory will in part be paid through the fulfillment of plans of the Patriotic Foundation to erect in Chicago a monument which will portray Salomon with his fellow patriots, George Washington and Robert Morris. I bespeak for the undertaking the fullest measure of success."

In urging honor to Haym Salomon, Roosevelt was in accord with the view of several of his predecessors. Taft, Harding, Coolidge, and Hoover also had deplored the failure of historians to include Salomon in the roster of Revolutionary War patriots.

August 24, 1936

My dear Mr. Hodes:

I am indeed gratified to learn that belated
recognition is to be made of the invaluable services
rendered to the cause of the American Revolution by
Haym Salomon. History was for a long time strangely
silent concerning the unselfish and munificent financial
support accorded the struggling colonies by this Philadelphia banker.

It was never disputed that at a critical period
in the affairs of the Revolution, Haym Salomon came to
the rescue of the Continental Congress with large loans
freely extended. The debt of gratitude which the Nation
owes Salomon's memory will in part be paid through the
fulfillment of plans of the Patriotic Foundation to erect
in Chicago a monument which will portray Salomon with his
fellow patriots, George Washington and Robert Morris. I
bespeak for the undertaking the fullest measure of success.

Very sincerely yours,

Franklin D Roosevelt

Mr. Barnet Hodes,
Co-Chairman of the Patriotic Foundation of Chicago,
33 North LaSalle Street,
Chicago, Illinois.

Tucson, Arizona,
April 27, 1939.

Mr. Barnet Hodes, Co-Chairman,
   The Patriotic Foundation of Chicago,
     33 North LaSalle Street,
      Chicago, Illinois.

My dear Mr. Hodes:

     I have read with deep interest your
letter of April 19th regarding the monument
project of the Patriotic Foundation of Chicago,
and have been especially pleased to note that
the plan includes recognition in this form, for
the first time, of the services of Haym Salomon
in the Revolutionary War.

     Though an alien at the time, Salomon
embraced whole-heartedly the cause of the
struggling colonists. His business genius and
self-sacrificing financial aid at critical
moments were invaluable and contributed greatly
to the success of our arms. The vital part he
played is truly symbolic of that fine American
tradition in which we take such pride - that
all creeds and nationalities have shared in the
founding and growth of our country.

     It is most fitting that the figure of
Haym Salomon should appear with those of George
Washington and Robert Morris on the monument
that the Patriotic Foundation of Chicago proposes
to erect, and I extend to the foundation my best
wishes for the success of the undertaking.

          Sincerely yours,

          John J. Pershing

A United States senator from Missouri who was destined to be Roosevelt's successor in the White House, Harry S. Truman, wrote: "It is gratifying to learn that the City of Chicago is intending to honor Haym Salomon and Robert Morris.... Salomon has been completely overlooked by history and Morris has never received his just dues."

Herbert H. Lehman, then governor of New York, wrote of Salomon: "He was a fine patriot and his name should be linked with other great Americans in the grateful remembrance of their fellow citizens. I hope the project ... will receive full public support."

Alfred E. Smith, political leader: "Republics are notoriously ungrateful in their recognition of services rendered for the common good and it is therefore gratifying to know that ... the unselfish patriotic service of one of our earliest patriots, Haym Salomon, is to be made manifest to all the world. I think it is especially fitting that in this statue you expect to erect, Haym Salomon should stand side by side with the two famous men he so faithfully served during the Nation's darkest hour."

General of the Army John J. Pershing: "Though an alien at the time, Salomon embraced wholeheartedly the cause of the struggling colonists. His business genius and self-sacrificing aid at critical moments were invaluable and contributed greatly to the success of our arms. The vital part he played is truly symbolic of that fine American tradition in which we take such pride—that all creeds and nationalities have shared in the founding and growth of our country." General Pershing added, "It is most fitting that the figure of Haym Salomon should appear with those of George Washington and Robert Morris on the monument."

The Nobel prize novelist Sinclair Lewis: "I am delighted that the Patriotic Foundation are giving recognition not only to George Washington and to Robert Morris but to that equally great, yet shamefully neglected, hero of the Revolutionary War, Haym Salomon. It seems to me important for this country to recognize how many varied racial strains have been involved in its history from the beginning."

Frank Murphy, the Roman Catholic governor of Michigan, later a justice of the Supreme Court: "It is especially heartening in this day that appropriate acknowledgment is at last to be made of Haym Salomon's patriotic service.... We may regret that as a nation we have hitherto forgotten him, but let us hope that from this time onward his name will ever be ranged alongside those of Washington, Morris and the others whose united efforts led the colonists to independence."

United States senator William E. Borah of Idaho: "Anyone familiar with the history of the American revolution realizes that proper credit has never been given to Haym Salomon for the great service he rendered to the cause of American freedom. I am greatly pleased that recognition of his great services is to be given in proper fashion."

Governor Olin B. Johnston of South Carolina: "Often times, men who do not figure in the forefront, perform the most patriotic services to their community, state and nation. That was true of Haym Salomon. Despite the fact that he did not take an active part in the political or military affairs, the sacrifices he made, and services he rendered are not less important. I wish for those responsible for this worthy undertaking the greatest amount of success."

Such representative endorsements illustrate how effectively the project was bringing its purposes before the public.

Numerous fraternal and veterans' groups, including the Cook County Council of the American Legion, commended the project. Typical was a resolution adopted by Chicago Lodge No. 4 of the Elks, which emphasized that through the proposed monument "the truth will be symbolized dramatically that men of all creeds and nationalities fought side by side in the American War for Independence, contributing their lives and fortunes in order that there might be established our free and democratic nation."

Official resolutions of commendation were passed by the City Council of Chicago and the Illinois State Senate. There was much favorable attention from the press, nationally as well as locally.

In the *Chicago American* one of the city's prominent writers, Milton Mayer, emphasized an especially striking feature of the project. "Chicago is to have a new and unique statue of the Father of His Country—a statue of George Washington flanked by the two patriots who helped him finance the American Revolution. The statue will be the first ever made that does not depict Washington alone." This design was a conscious deviation from tradition to make the point that civilian-military cooperation was essential to Washington's success.

On the same theme an editorial in the *Chicago Daily News* said: "Chicago can be proud of its efforts in raising by public subscription a monument in memory of Haym Salomon. It will make up, a little, for the long neglect. Robert Morris and George Washington would be proud enough, we imagine, to share the statue with him, just as he was proud to share his lot and fortunes with them, in a day when a man counted as a man, whether Jew or Gentile, general or moneylender, financier or statesman."

The *Christian Century*, influential journal of religion, gave the project editorial commendation by describing the monument as "likely to prove an event of permanent social significance.... One is moved to meditate upon how meager a part of history gets into books of history and upon how rare it is for one, whose services, no matter how great, have not been of a conspicuous military or political kind, to be remembered." The editorial then commented: "The monument, to be the work of Lorado Taft, will not have as its primary object, however, the honoring of individuals as such but rather the celebrating of the fact that people of many races, appropriately symbolized by this Polish Jew, participated in the war for independence. Americans are accustomed to think of their country as one in which many nationalities have found a home; it is important that we be reminded that a number of these nationalities were present from the very beginning and helped lay the foundation of the republic. The United States not only has become much more than an Anglo-Saxon people; it has been such from the start."

The good start that such favorable attention meant was shadowed by the death of Lorado Taft on October 30, 1936. He had suffered a paralyzing stroke the previous week while engaged in putting some finishing touches to his model of the monument.

Taft had a premonition that he was dying, and the Washington–Morris–Salomon monument was much on his mind. With a death-bed wish he asked Professor Douglas to make certain that the model he had created would be realized in bronze. Douglas communicated Taft's wish to Hodes and other officials of the Patriotic Foundation and was told to assure the artist that the monument would be completed. A day later death came to Lorado Taft.

The foundation made a decision that the monument should be completed as a Lorado Taft creation. The figures of the three patriots would be realized by a group of artists, known as the Lorado Taft Associates, who had worked closely with Taft. Leonard Crunelle, from his boyhood a protege of Taft's, whose relationship to Taft had been like that of a son, would complete the sculpture. He had the status of a recognized sculptor in his own right after the National Commission of Fine Arts earlier awarded him a $50,000 prize, but he pledged himself, out of loyalty to his patron, to follow Taft's model and designs, and information gained in discussions with him. Both the foundation and Mrs. Taft were satisfied that Crunelle would produce a work Lorado Taft could have called his own. And that he did. On the right end of the bronze base is etched, "Designed by Lorado Taft, Sc."

Completion took longer than expected not only for artistic reasons but because the various phases, such as casting the upright figures, creating the bronze plaque across the rear of the base, and cutting the forty-ton granite base, had to be paced with the progress of the fund raising.

A great dinner was held in May 1939 in the grand ballroom of Chicago's Conrad Hilton Hotel (then known as the Stevens). Haym Salomon was represented at the speakers' table by a flag-draped empty chair. Also at the speakers' table were Mayor Edward J. Kelly; Bishop (later Archbishop) Bernard J. Sheil of the Roman Catholic Church; Rabbi Michael Aaronsohn, blinded war veteran and former national chaplain of the Disabled American Veterans; and Dr. Duncan Browne, rector of St. James' Episcopal Church of Chicago.

Alben W. Barkley, later vice-president but then majority leader of the United States Senate, was the main speaker at the dinner. He gave a characteristically stirring oration on the theme of Haym Salomon as a symbol of American democracy in operation. Nearly one thousand Chicagoans attended and saw the premiere of a two-reel motion picture in color, *Sons of Liberty*. That picture produced by Warner Brothers with Claude

Rains portraying Salomon was later seen by hundreds of thousands of persons across the nation.

The impressive program was climaxed by Barnet Hodes announcement, $50,000 for the monument had been raised. The word go could be given for all phases of the work begun by Lorado Taft to be completed.

19
Dedication

The monument was legally conveyed to the city of Chicago on June 19, 1941, when the City Council adopted a resolution accepting it. At the same time Heald Square at Wacker drive and Wabash avenue was designated as its site.

This prominent site in downtown Chicago was suggested by Mayor Kelly. He wrote the City Council that the monument, because of its significance and artistic nature, deserved "the highest position our City is able to bestow upon it." The same view was expressed editorially by the *Chicago Herald American:*

> A monument that so perfectly symbolizes the spirit of American unity and tolerance should be where ALL Chicagoans can see it as they come and go, so that their own faith in America and their gratitude for this priceless boon of BEING AMERICANS may be daily renewed.

Aside from general antidemocratic agitation in the world there was urgent reason for emphasis on American unity. The new World War had been touched off by Hitler's invasion of Poland in 1939. Although the United States was not yet at war, it was on the alert with a program of national defense. The Mayor's communication to the City Council said:

> It is important—indeed, it is vital—that in these days we demonstrate to the nation, and to the world, that America's second largest city is united and resolved to protect and defend our democracy. Our national defense is as much a matter of spirit as it is of production, as much of moral quality as a physical one.
>
> For this reason, the monument established by the Patriotic Foundation of Chicago assumes an even greater importance in the cultural life of our city. It can stand, and will stand, as Chicago's testimonial to the hardiness of the democratic spirit.

December 15, 1941, had been designated by Congress and proclaimed by President Roosevelt as *Bill of Rights Day* for a nationwide celebration of the 150th anniversary of the adoption of the first ten amendments to the Constitution of the United States. The dedication ceremony was planned as part of Chicago's salute to the Bill of Rights. But eight days before on Sunday, December 7, Pearl Harbor had been attacked by Japan. The United States was at war.

Thus, when unveiled to reveal the larger-than-life figures of Washington and his co-patriots, the monument stood with more immediate meaning than had been envisioned. The symbol of America as a nation of freedom for all regardless of origin or religion became a symbol of what was required then, full support by civilians for

the military forces. This inevitable theme of the dedication was implicit in a second message concerning the
monument that President Roosevelt had sent for the
dedication:

November 13, 1941

My dear Mr. Hodes:

    The strength of the American cause in the War
of the Revolution lay in the fact that in every critical
phase of the contest the right leaders were raised up to
perform whatever task needed to be done.

    The incomparable leadership of Washington would
have been nullified without the able support he received
from key men in the various stages of the struggle out of
which we emerged as a Nation.

    Two financiers on whom Washington leaned heavily
in the darkest hours of the Revolution were Haym Salomon
and Robert Morris. Their genius in finance and fiscal
affairs and unselfish devotion to the cause of liberty
made their support of the utmost importance when the
struggling colonies were fighting against such heavy odds.

    It is, therefore, especially appropriate that
this great triumvirate of patriots -- George Washington,
Robert Morris and Haym Salomon -- should be commemorated
together in Chicago. The memorial which you are about to
dedicate will stand as an inspiration to generations yet
unborn to place love of country above every selfish end.

            Very sincerely yours,

            Franklin D. Roosevelt

Honorable Barnet Hodes,
Co-Chairman,
Patriotic Foundation of Chicago,
Chicago, Illinois.

THE WHITE HOUSE
WASHINGTON

September 3, 1941

Dear Mr. Hodes:

I was greatly interested to
learn that the project sponsored by
the Patriotic Foundation of Chicago
is reaching fruition and that the
monument, symbolizing a fundamental
fact of American tolerance, soon will
be dedicated. Please convey my congratulations to all those who have
contributed to the success of this
undertaking.

Very sincerely yours,

Eleanor Roosevelt

Colonel Sprague, who presided at the dedication, said:

> In the history of our nation, there never has been a time when we have been threatened, or when a call to the colors was made, that men of all nationalities, colors, races, or creeds did not rally to the support of our flag.

In particular does Haym Salomon stand for that historic truth.

Hodes formally presented the monument to the people of the city of Chicago. He said:

> They tell us—Robert Morris and Haym Salomon —that civilian cooperation, and, yes, civilian sacrifice, with the military and naval forces was no less important in the first days of our Republic than it is today. Joined with the indomitable Washington, they will stand here to remind us that America became the America we love because there was that working together between civilians and soldiers without which no war can be won.
>
> It is the fervent hope of those who made this monument possible that all who see it, today and through the years to come, will catch from it and be constantly inspired by this crucial lesson from the past.

Freedom and tolerance were not forgotten as Hodes added: "This monument symbolizes the great American principles which make our land doubly worth defending. The single word Freedom is almost enough by itself to describe those principles."

This same concept was emphasized by military as well as civilian speakers at the dedication, for example, Major General Joseph M. Cummins, commander of the Sixth Corps of the Army:

It is particularly appropriate today that all Americans realize the priceless treasures we have in our Bill of Rights. It is fitting that we take time to appreciate, cherish and stand united to preserve that Bill of Rights, that priceless heritage—freedom of religion, of speech, of the press, and of assembly and petition—which was bought at a high price in the blood of another generation of Americans and is worth any price to keep in trust for our future American citizens.

Captain E. A. Lofquist, chief of staff of the Great Lakes Naval Station, said of the First Amendment freedoms: "That is America. And it is those things which must not die."

Similar sentiments were expressed by clergymen of the Protestant, Roman Catholic, and Jewish faiths.

Bishop Wallace E. Conkling of the Episcopal Diocese of Chicago spoke of democracy.

Democracy is based upon the faith and the hope that there is *something* in man—upon the conviction that man is worthy of being given rights and liberties—that he will rise up to fulfill such privileges—that he will answer to such challenging responsibilities.

The Reverend William I. Bergin, representing Bishop Bernard J. Sheil, in extolling the Bill of Rights expressed the hope that "to the four great freedoms enunciated in the first Bill of Rights there will be added two more freedoms . . . freedom from fear and freedom from want."

Rabbi Abraham A. Neuman of congregation Mikveh Israel, Haym Salomon's synagogue in Philadelphia (introduced by Chicago's Rabbi Morris Teller) illustrated the meaning of the monument by recalling an ancient Hebrew legend.

When God was about to create man from the dust of the earth, he gathered the precious dust from all parts of the earth, the East and the West, the North and the South, so that no country may at some future time say: of us alone did God create the human race. The same American conception of human brotherhood is revealed in eloquent form by this monument.

Our nation is one. . . . All elements of the world's population . . . have entered into the making of the American people. Indeed, no day is more fitting for utterance of this truth than this day consecrated to the Bill of Rights. What the Ten Commandments proclaimed on Sinai, what the Sermon on the Mount has meant for Christian civilizations, the Bill of Rights has expressed in terms of human rights for the society of men and the democratic way of life.

Governor Dwight H. Green of Illinois, United States Senator Scott W. Lucas of Illinois, and Mayor Kelly also participated in the dedication ceremonies. The mayor observed:

George Washington and his friend, Robert Morris, were Christians. Haym Salomon was a Jew. . . . These three, though of widely different walks of life, labored together in a common cause in order that the American way of life, as we know it today, might be guaranteed to future generations of other Americans, the right to live as free men, knowing no master, alive to their own opportunities, yet tolerant and sympathetic toward others. To my mind, this typifies the very spirit of America.

Governor Green said:

> From this magnificent monument comes the eloquent appeal to all Americans never to surrender their birthright of liberty, tolerance and equality. ... Given to us from the hands of the sculptor is portrayal of the spirit of tolerance which has bound Americans together in a brotherhood of freedom. We see Christian clasping hands with Jew, each acknowledging the equality of the other, and united in a common purpose. They represented two faiths, but they were concerned only in breaking the bonds which thwarted the concepts of freedom of speech, freedom of opportunity and freedom of religious worship.

In the same vein Senator Lucas referred to the three figures on the monument as representing

> the ideals we reaffirm in a challenging world. ... Different as day and night, yet these three men held as one the torch of liberty, worshipping God, each in his own way, each daring the hangman tyrant's halter in the cause of that new light of the world—democracy. ... From this monument we take courage and hope. We rise in the image of these three men to shield the light of liberty from extinction, to keep our country what they helped to make it—the permanent abode of sacred freedoms, the greatest of which is the freedom of man's religious soul.

The monument itself most eloquently expresses the great theme of freedom, particularly through the figure of Haym Salomon. Everyone in the throng at the dedication ceremony, standing in the open air on a bitter cold day reminiscent of Valley Forge, must have been impressed.

A great and much-beloved Chicago editor, Richard J. Finnegan, captured the significance of the dedication in the *Chicago Times*,

> It is almost awesomely splendid that America happens to honor Haym Salomon on this day when once again we are engaged in a struggle for man's liberties . . . against a tyranny so rotten that it has had to bolster its false courage by cruel persecution of the race which gave us Haym Salomon.

The *Chicago Sun*, launched only a few days before by Chicago's Marshall Field (and later merged with the *Times*) concluded an editorial headed *Symbol of Faith:* "Chicago rejoices in a new monument . . . especially that Haym Salomon has at last been fittingly honored. He belongs there with Washington and Morris."

20
The Story Continues

The story of the monument did not end with its somber yet inspiring dedication on that wartime day of 1941, which was but a climax in a continuing story. The message of American principles is projected by the mere existence of the monument.

Since 1941 hundreds of thousands of persons, men, women, and most important, children, have seen it. That the Jewish name Haym Salomon has been lodged in the consciousness of America as a name that stands for patriotism is a safe assumption. History books and encyclopedias which did not mention Salomon before now tell his story. Newspaper and magazine articles about Salomon have appeared frequently. In December 1967, as an example, the magazine *Commerce*, published by the Chicago Association of Commerce and Industry, devoted its cover to a painting of the monument. In 1970 the new All-American Bank of Chicago, which especially serves people of various ethnic stocks, adopted the monument as its symbol.

In fact, Haym Salomon is no longer news as a Revolutionary War patriot, but the foundation does want the monument to continue to be *in* the news—getting the story told to each new generation. Thus the foundation has itself inspired or cooperated with other agencies in events that center attention on the monument or on Haym Salomon.

When American Masonic Heritage Week was celebrated in 1962, a major phase of the observance was a ceremony at the monument. A lighting system had been installed to illuminate the monument effectively at night, and it was turned on by a button that set off a signal at the monument. President John F. Kennedy, whose election as the first Roman Catholic in the White House accorded with the principles of the Patriotic Foundation, pressed that button while visiting in Michigan.

On December 15, 1966, there was an observance of the 175th anniversary of the Bill of Rights and the 25th anniversary of the dedication of the monument with Mayor Richard J. Daley participating. Each year on Washington's birthday there is a wreath-laying ceremony at the monument.

This publicity is all to the good. The historic truth that the United States is a nation of many kinds of people and has been so from the beginning needs constant reiteration. Prejudice seems to be something always latent, a poisonous element in nation, state, city, and community. America has not escaped the effects of the poison. There were the Know-nothing politicians and the era of the Ku Klux Klan. Even Nazism had some admirers and adherents in America. But like the sentries of Washington's troops the monument in Heald Square stands on guard—a symbol of the true America.

For Mr. Barney Hodies —
with best regards —
John F. Kennedy

President Kennedy also hailed
the monument to "this great
trimvirate of patriots." In
1962, from Michigan, he pushed
button that turned on lighting.

104

Affirming that the monument is a civic landmark, Chicago Mayor Daley joined 1962 observance. Judge Norman Eiger is behind the Mayor. Barnet Hodes is at right.